GATHER
COOK
FEAST

JESSICA SEATON
AND ANNA COLQUHOUN

GATHER
COOK
FEAST

RECIPES FROM LAND AND WATER
BY THE CO-FOUNDER OF TOAST

PHOTOGRAPHY BY
JONATHAN LOVEKIN AND NICK SEATON

FIG TREE
an imprint of
PENGUIN BOOKS

FIG TREE

UK | USA | Canada | Ireland | Australia
India | New Zealand | South Africa

Fig Tree is part of the Penguin Random House group of companies
whose addresses can be found at global.penguinrandomhouse.com.

First published 2017
001

Designed by Charlotte Heal Design
Colour reproduction by Rhapsody London
Printed in China

A CIP catalogue record for this book is available from the British Library

ISBN: 978–0–241–21609–5

www.greenpenguin.co.uk

To my mum, who filled
our home with a love of food

GATHER COOK FEAST

A PLATE THAT FEELS LIKE A PLACE

I only ever wanted to live in nature. I grew up in fields, messing about in streams, learning about flowers, nestled in a hedge bank with a book. As soon as I could after graduating I moved with my husband, Jamie, to West Wales, one of the wilder parts of Britain, where the coast is tortuous, long and never far away, the population sparse and the wooded river valleys full of wild flowers. There I learned to forage, to gather mushrooms in the woods, to make nettle soup and to pick wild garlic.

I shouldn't paint this existence as a pastoral idyll. In the mess of a working and family life, all this pure escapism is reduced to the functional day to day. But I have often wanted to represent an affinity with a particular place and landscape in my work, first when Jamie and I were designing and making knitwear, then more recently in our invention of the Toast brand and the associated goods and shops you may know today. In the expansive final stages of many long upland walks, our tongues loosened by exercise, I have long dreamed and sketched out plans for a recipe book about place.

This is a book about landscape and food, about imagining food that, in some way, both comes from and represents landscape. A plate that feels like a place, if you will.

I am interested in the idea that a deep, intense human love of something may prompt a desire to savour and connect with the mouth and lips: the feeling of wanting to 'eat it all up'. The passion we may have for our natural world can be recreated afresh by tasting the salty essence of sea marsh in samphire, or savouring feelings of cold uplands in pine jelly, or perhaps enjoying anew the residual warmth of late summer in toasted hay potatoes.

On these islands, many of us enjoy an intimate relationship with landscape and the natural world. Stitched into our psyche is an obsession with weather; we find a soothing connection with untrammelled nature when listening to the shipping forecast. Our cultural life is peppered with representations of our land through artists such as Constable, Nash, Nicholson and at times even Hockney, while the literature and poetry of Ted Hughes, Heaney, Hardy and Muir is underpinned by a connection with the (not always cosy) nature of our rich and varied landscape. There are countless such examples. This is our heritage and part of who we still are.

I have no qualifications as a professional cook. This has been a long journey for me (over four years from initial idea to fruition). I come from a family of enthusiastic cooks, learning with my sister and brother at my mother's side. In our home food was celebrated, my mum keen and open to try new tastes and ingredients, her food always delicious. Responding, my dad brought home the first avocado we had seen – rock hard, taut and intensely green, turning it over in his hand without a thought of what to do with it. Mum taught us joy in food, cooking appetizing food daily and often making simple ad hoc picnics of good red wine, bread and roast chicken. In Italy, lacking the language and not caring how she would appear, she used hilarious mime and gesture to buy those ingredients for us to eat on a sleeper train journey back home through the Alps. She always cooked from scratch when other mums fell gratefully on Vesta chicken curries to soothe the drudgery of the homemaker. Later, in my own home, she would lean over my shoulder while I was at the cooker and ask what I was making and how and why.

I have been very fortunate that my idea of representing landscape in food was taken up with great enthusiasm by Anna Colquhoun – an experienced professional chef and culinary anthropologist and my collaborator on this project – who totally understood and empathized with my ideas from the start. She has guided me in my inexperience and informed the whole process. I have learned so much and I couldn't have made this book without her.

Now most of us live in cities, landscape and wilderness play a lesser role in our lives. Our struggles are not those of wrenching a livelihood from an impersonal, wild and intractable environment. We have tamed the land and stripped the sea and bent them to our will. But perhaps now – because of this new reality – there is a need to feel it more.

Thus there is a great and very positive groundswell happening in the world of food: young and not-so-young women and men, very bright and committed and hard-working, have set up small hands-on businesses. Artisanal bakers in railway arches; cheese makers in country barns; biodynamic vegetable growers; brewers; salmon smokers; distillers; free-range pig farmers; mutton-producing hill farms; collectively run cafés and restaurants popping up in unlikely buildings. These aren't coldly planned money-making enterprises but inspired individuals operating from a love of what they're doing.

Perhaps this groundswell is, in part, an expression of this human desire to reconnect with the soil, with the wholesome fundamentals of human existence. But, however laudable, these movements are not yet mainstream, the target audience select, often moneyed. The greater challenge is to feed our peoples well without environmental damage and degradation. This book does not seek to answer this complex question, but perhaps we can at least remind ourselves that, after all, landscape and food and humanity are all part of one giant, entirely interconnected system.

My natural style of cooking is loose and experimental and often consists of a selection of simply prepared ingredients in one bowl, but I also enjoy preparing more elaborate food for friends and family. Gathering around a table with those you love, to share wholesome, tasty food along with good conversation, is a deep joy. I wanted the book to reflect this range. So there is a base of easy meals to make after a busy day, interspersed with a few very short recipes typical of my style and some celebratory dishes for significant gatherings. I have also included a few projects to explore – hot-smoking, sausage making and bacon curing, and the art of sourdough baking are a few. I hope you will feel encouraged to try and will enjoy the achievement of slicing and cooking your own bacon or nursing a sourdough to life – cooking as a beautiful pleasure.

I do hope you enjoy reading, cooking and, most importantly, eating the food from this book.

ABOUT THE RECIPES

This book divides the recipes into loosely conceived sections relating to types of landscape. When I imagine these landscapes, I imagine them in the British Isles, but they could equally be transferred to similar landscapes in France, Connecticut or any other temperate land.

In putting this book together I also imagined an association of season with each landscape and its foods. So the book starts with fresh, new growth of early spring in the Freshwater section and moves through the year to conclude with winter in the Upland section and its more sustaining foods. This was pure instinct and sprang from personal enthusiasm – to associate woods with the mushrooms and nuts of autumn, rather than the wild garlic of spring, just felt right.

Inevitably, the boundaries of season and place are smudgy and I make no apologies for the fact that spring vegetables accompany the duck in a pot when wild duck cannot be found in spring (unless frozen), or that I chose beef for the Field & Pasture section and sheep for the Upland section, whereas both can be found grazing in fields. I have taken poetic licence.

I don't mean to berate the cook when I mention how to present a dish within the recipes – of course you will make your own choices – but I do find presentation of food on a carefully chosen plate very important and will often make suggestions. For me it adds to the pleasure and sense of occasion when taste, smell and look go hand in hand. And small details can make all the difference.

I prefer to buy organic produce wherever I can, mostly because of the positive impact on biodiversity usually afforded by growing

organically. But I haven't been prescriptive about organic grown.
I do favour British suppliers – the spirit of this book is about place after all – but not exclusively; ingredients are chosen because of their intrinsic qualities, rather than because of a slavish adherence to 'all British'.

In the recipes where it is relevant, I have given a note of guidance for seasonality in key ingredients. The months given are, by necessity, just a guide. The moment of peak ripeness of any fruit or vegetable, the appearance of shoals of fish, or the perfect time to cull game is dependent on a huge number of factors – the weather that year; movement of tides and currents; an individual farmer's situation and the breed or variety of the produce in question; all of these factors play a part in the moment a particular item comes to market.

In this book, the months quoted in the recipes reflect the typical peak season for that produce, in the British Isles.

There are a few ingredients of note:
— Sea salt is always specified, both because it is directly extracted from sea water (so is more appropriate to the spirit of this book) and because of its higher levels of trace elements. Choose a fine grade for general use, flaky when you need that specific crunch.
— Butter is unsalted, unless otherwise stated.
— Eggs should always be truly free-range or organic.
— Lemons are usually unwaxed, especially when the zest is needed.

This book also introduces some unfamiliar ingredients, some foraged ones and many that are more familiar. I'd like to bring some of these less familiar ingredients into more common use – the British pea and bean, the herring, seaweed. Where it isn't crucial to the recipe, I have tried wherever possible to suggest substitutions. Where it would change the nature of the recipe, I have held my nerve.

More information on sourcing this more unusual produce is given at the back of the book.

A WORD ON FORAGING

This book intentionally uses a selection of foraged ingredients. Mostly this is because it's an enjoyable, grounding practice: getting out into the open air and eating foodstuffs packed with nutrition and complex compounds bred out of many domestic cultivars. One of the several theories to explain the long life of residents on the Greek island of Ikaria is that foraging and eating spring weeds provides both complex nutrition and exercise to the islanders.

The act of foraging provides a direct connection between you and the way the plant, mushroom or seaweed grows. It connects you with habitat and the importance of a biodiverse environment and with how our ancestors have picked and gathered for millennia.

For detailed instruction in the whys and wherefores of foraging, check the Further Reading & Learning section at the back of the book, to study in more depth, or – even better – to attend a course where you can learn directly from a teacher to hold, smell and taste plants and fungi without risk.

In order to forage safely you have to 'know' a plant, mushroom or seaweed in a way that goes beyond the tick box of colour, height, habitat or smell. This sort of knowing is similar to how you can instinctively tell your partner or child apart from others at a distance, because of gait, shape or stance. This takes time and persistence. In truth there are few poisonous plants or fungi to confuse, but certain plant or mushroom families have more than others (the Umbellifer family is one), so it is wise to learn these well. Additionally, some plants may contain compounds that are best consumed in small quantities (although, unknown to many, so do some shop-bought foodstuffs – apricot kernels, for example) or they may need heat to neutralize. Learning is important.

If the intention is to preserve habitat and biodiversity, then sustainability is a given. No digging roots (illegal in any case without landowners' permission), picking judiciously without stripping all growth and generally following guidance given by experts. It is not an offence to gather plants for personal use, but tact and a considerate approach are essential. Don't wander on land without permission and don't forage on protected sites (Sites of Special Scientific Interest or National Nature Reserves). It's wise to avoid sites that may be polluted, alongside busy roads, in parks frequented by dogs and among fields where crops have been sprayed.

You may choose to buy some of the foraged ingredients specified and there are some sources on pages 334–6 to help you do that.

Lastly, it is very important to be aware that gathering wild food may impact population sizes of some foraged foods. Be respectful and gather judiciously. The more people value diverse habitats and are vocal in support of a varied and rich flora and fauna, the more foods will be available for future foragers.

ROCK DAMP FLUVIAL
CRAYFISH GREEN
CARP PERCH SHADE
COOL **FRESHWATER**
NARROWS TROUT

WEEDS WATERCRESS
MEANDER SILT RILL
GARLIC EDDY
MALLARD NETTLES
DEEP RICE SPROUT

Our rivers and lakes are the lifeblood of the land. They comprise complex ecologies of flora and fauna, providing much of the freshwater we need as well as somewhere for fishing, wild swimming and stone skimming. This section is a celebration of our still and flowing waters; of the fish that swim there; of the herbs and plants that flourish nearby and of the wildfowl that paddle the waters.

Latterly, among the many edible freshwater fish only salmon, sea trout and trout are popular in Britain. But there are more species suitable for eating, such as the American signal crayfish, pike-perch and farmed carp (which needs no fishmeal to thrive). Medieval monks would keep fishponds to supply their Friday suppers. Perhaps we may learn to love freshwater fish more widely, as they do in Central Europe, and take a little pressure off the seas.

Early spring brings new growth: fresh green shoots in the wild and in the garden. Chives come first, then nettles, mint, wild garlic, sorrel, lovage. Many of these herbs love shade and water. After months of relative cold and darkness, this new growth is charged with vital antioxidants and vitamins. Lovage, in particular, is a very under-used herb. Strong and lusty, the quantity employed should be approached with caution, but a little finely chopped lovage adds a complex, earthy, celery flavour to soups, salads and cooked vegetables. Spring is also a time for the first foraged leaves: nettles, wild garlic, dandelion and many others.

Around the world festivals have evolved to celebrate spring, often centred around spring growth. For Greeks the gathering of wild greens as a spring ritual is still alive, whether they still live on an island or have decamped to California. In Iran, the New Year festival is celebrated on the spring equinox with *sabzi polo mahi*, rice cooked with lots of herbs and served with fish. From Germany to Slovakia, Maundy Thursday is called 'Green Thursday' and often only green vegetables are eaten on this day. In this section you will find new responses to these traditions.

Chilled Six Leaf Soup

SERVES 6

60g butter
6 spring onions, white and pale
    green parts only, thinly sliced
2 leeks, white and pale green
    parts only, thinly sliced
    (around 300g prepared)
fine sea salt
2 cloves of garlic, peeled
    and very finely chopped
2 medium potatoes, peeled
    and cut into 1cm cubes
    (around 300g prepared)
100g watercress leaves,
    roughly chopped
100g baby spinach leaves,
    roughly chopped
100g tender nettle tips,
    roughly chopped
a small bunch of chives, chopped
150ml double cream
2–3 teaspoons finely grated
    fresh horseradish (or prepared
    horseradish from a jar)

To finish
100ml double cream, lightly whipped
a grating of horseradish
several reserved chives, finely snipped

This show-stopper bright green soup exudes vitality and soft creaminess in the same spoonful. The combination of peppery watercress and horseradish stands in for black pepper. The almost raw leaves add a punch of nutrition – iron, folic acid, vitamins and antioxidants. If you prefer not to include nettles, add an extra 50g each of watercress and spinach.

Melt the butter in a saucepan, then add the spring onions, leeks and a pinch of salt and soften over a low to medium heat, stirring occasionally, without letting the vegetables take colour. Add the garlic and soften for another minute or two.

Add the potatoes, 500ml of cold water and another generous pinch of salt and cover. Increase the heat to bring to a boil, then reduce the heat and simmer until the potatoes are tender, around 15 minutes.

Turn off the heat, then add the watercress, spinach, nettle tips and chives (save a few for the top) and stir until they wilt. Transfer the soup to a wide bowl, add 400ml of ice-cold water and leave to cool as quickly as possible (this fast cooling preserves the bright green colour).

Blend the soup until really smooth, using a jug blender or immersion blender. Then stir in the 150ml of double cream. Take out a ladleful of the soup and put it into a small bowl, whisk in 2 teaspoons of the horseradish, then transfer back into the soup. Thin the soup with more cold water if it is too thick.

Taste the soup and add more horseradish or salt if you need it.

Serve the soup chilled, with a spoonful of whipped cream, a grating of horseradish and a few finely snipped chives on the top.

Watercress Salad with Blood Oranges & Popped Wild Rice

SERVES 4 AS A SMALL
PLATE, 2 HUNGRY PEOPLE

4 large bulb spring onions,
    green and tough parts removed,
    sliced into rounds
juice of ½ a blood orange
sea salt
2 teaspoons sunflower oil
20g wild rice
1–2 teaspoons sumac powder,
    depending on strength
200g watercress, washed and
    spun dry, large stems removed
2 small blood oranges,
    peeled, scraped of pith,
    sliced into thin discs
6 fat red radishes, quartered,
    with stems trimmed
150g Feta, crumbled

The dressing
1 tablespoon cider vinegar
2 tablespoons olive oil
sea salt and black pepper

I have never found wild watercress – it doesn't grow where I live – but by reputation its peppery hit is a significant cut above the (often limp) bags found in the supermarket.

Here is a salad to make with the best cultivated watercress you can find, paired with the last of the blood oranges and the first little radishes and spring onions. The innovation here is nutty wild rice (from another water-loving plant), popped out of its shiny black jacket in an almost dry pan and then dusted with tangy sumac and some salt. It's good as a tasty, crunchy snack too.

Put the prepared spring onions into a bowl, squeeze the blood orange juice over and add a grinding of sea salt, then mix all together and leave for 10 minutes.

Now pop the wild rice. Before you start, spread some double layers of kitchen paper on the side ready to take the popped rice.

Take a heavy, wide, lidded pan, pour in the sunflower oil and put on a high heat until shimmering and hot. Scatter a portion of the wild rice into the hot oil – you want it to have plenty of room to move, so each grain has good contact with the heat. Clamp the lid on tightly until you hear the rice starting to pop against the lid. Take the pan off the heat and keep shaking it until the popping sound stops. Carefully lift the lid and check all the rice is popped (there's a fine line between ready and spoilt). Spread the popped rice out on the kitchen paper. Continue in batches until all the rice is popped. Then pour into a bowl and dust with the sumac and a pinch or two of salt to taste.

Put the watercress into a big bowl, then whisk the dressing and pour over, tossing to incorporate. Add the rounds of spring onion with the juice, scatter over the rounds of blood orange and the radishes, then sprinkle over the sumac-dusted popped wild rice and the crumbled Feta.

Dandelion, Quail's Egg
& Bacon Salad

SERVES 4 AS A LIGHT LUNCH
OR SMALL PLATE

80g tender whole dandelion
    leaves, washed and spun dry
1 tablespoon olive oil
8 rashers of unsmoked streaky
    bacon, rind removed
12 quail's eggs, at room temperature

The mustard vinaigrette
1 tablespoon cider vinegar
2 tablespoons olive oil
1 teaspoon Dijon mustard
sea salt and black pepper

LATE MARCH TO EARLY JULY
FOR WILD DANDELIONS

A quick and delicious early spring salad, where meltingly soft eggs and salty bacon offset the bitter leaves. Tender leaves are important for this salad, or some peppery wild rocket could substitute (see foraging info on page 337).

Make the vinaigrette by whisking all the ingredients together.

Put the prepared dandelion leaves into a generous bowl. Using the olive oil, brown the bacon in a heavy pan, over a medium heat, until crisp. Remove from the pan and keep warm. Deglaze the pan with the mustard vinaigrette.

Place a pan of water on the heat and bring to the boil. When boiling, gently lower the quail's eggs into the water and boil for 2½ minutes for a softly runny set. Add another minute if you prefer them hard-boiled.

Have ready a bath of cold water. When the eggs are done, remove them with a slotted spoon and lower them into the cold water. Here you can easily peel the shells from the eggs. Try to do this quickly, so that the eggs are still gently warm once you've finished. Once the eggs are peeled, cut them all in half. Chop the warm bacon into 2cm pieces and scatter over the leaves.

Warm the vinaigrette in the pan for a brief moment, then dribble over the salad and toss to combine. Add the halved eggs as a topping. Serve quickly before the leaves go limp.

Some good crusty bread alongside will mop up the juices.

GATHER COOK FEAST

Wet Garlic &
New Potato Soup

SERVES 4 AS A SMALL BOWL,
2 HUNGRY PEOPLE FOR SUPPER

2 or 3 heads of wet garlic,
    depending on their size
1 small leek
1 bunch of spring onions
    (about 6 onions)
1 pale stick of celery
50g butter
sea salt and black pepper
400g new potatoes (or salad
    potatoes), scrubbed and
    cut into small cubes
500ml good-quality vegetable
    or chicken stock
125g crème fraîche
leaves from a small bunch
    of fresh mint, sliced into
    ribbons at the last minute
a small bunch of chives, chopped
a pinch of sugar (optional)

LATE SPRING TO EARLY
SUMMER FOR WET GARLIC

Wet garlic belongs to the watery, green, fresh-growth-feel of rivers and ferny banks. It is found from late May to June, when the autumn-sown garlic has swelled in the increasing light and warmth, but before the sun has had a chance to dry the skin to papery whiteness. In this pale green, waxy and juicy state more of the garlic bulb can be eaten – you only need peel away the slightly drier outer layer and perhaps the very top of the stem and you can cook the rest. The key to success with this fresh, gentle and sumptuous soup is chopping the ingredients very finely and keeping the soup fresh by softening them in the pan without caramelizing. Lovely too served cold the next day, maybe with an extra dollop of crème fraîche and chives, or some finely sliced, salted and peppered cucumber on the top.

Peel and trim the garlic as above, then cut each bulb and its stem in half lengthways and slice the stems into very fine half-moons. Divide each section of bulb (again lengthways) into three or four segments, stopping your knife just short of the root base so that it remains held together in one piece. Now slice perpendicular to these cuts, across the bulb, very finely, so that the garlic is reduced to a pile of small thin pieces.

Prepare the leek in a similar way. Remove the dark green part. Cut the leek in half lengthways and flush out any dirt trapped between the leaves. Make two or three lengthways cuts, stopping just short of the root end, and then slice crossways as finely as you can. Slice the spring onions finely and reserve the dark green pieces for garnish. Divide the celery into two or three pieces lengthways, slicing it like the leek and garlic. Melt the butter in a heavy-based saucepan over a medium-low heat. Add the garlic, leek, spring onions and celery along with a pinch of salt and soften slowly, stirring occasionally, for 15–20 minutes – don't let them colour.

Add the diced potatoes and cook for a further 5 minutes, then pour over the stock and bring to the boil. Cover, reduce the heat and let simmer gently until the potatoes are tender, 10–15 minutes. If it seems too thick, add a dash of water. Remove from the heat and stir in the crème fraîche and prepared herbs. Taste and season generously with salt and pepper. A pinch of sugar will help balance the garlicky flavour should you be inclined. Serve with some of the sliced dark green spring onion leaves.

Asparagus Risotto with Sorrel & Wild Garlic

SERVES 4

2 litres vegetable stock,
    chicken stock or water
500g asparagus
30g wild garlic leaves
30g sorrel leaves
2 bunches of spring onions,
    trimmed of roots and
    damaged bits (12 or so)
175ml sunflower oil
sea salt and black pepper
80g butter
4 cloves of garlic, peeled
    and very finely chopped
350g good risotto rice
300ml dry, crisp white wine
80g Parmesan, finely grated

MAY FOR FLOWERING WILD
GARLIC, FROM EARLY SPRING FOR
WILD OR CULTIVATED SORREL

In early spring sorrel starts to push up through the earth. This admirable plant has great vigour at the start, before the slugs get going and the wind starts to tatter the leaves. Its supple, soft, spear-shaped leaves have a lemony sour-green taste which here combines with the wild garlic in a bright fresh sauce – a good spring-like contrast to the soothing, creamy asparagus risotto.

Using only warm oil to make the herb sauce avoids sorrel's natural tendency to army khaki when it gets really hot under the collar.

To use entirely foraged herbs, hunt for wild common sorrel (*Rumex acetosa*). As the name implies, it is common throughout the country and is sour, intense and very delicious. Once you know this plant you'll find yourself grabbing a leaf to chew on a long walk – invigorating and refreshing. Both wild garlic and sorrel can be shop-bought.

Bring the stock to a simmer in a saucepan. Snap off the tough ends of the asparagus and give them each a thwack, using the flat of your knife, to crush them. Add them to the pan and simmer for around 15 minutes to flavour the stock, then remove.

To make the herb oil: roughly chop the wild garlic, sorrel and around one-third of the spring onions' dark green tops. Heat the sunflower oil over a low flame until warm. Blend the chopped leaves with the warm oil on high speed for several minutes, until really smooth. Sieve the oil, gently encouraging it through with the back of a spoon.

Cut the asparagus spears into 2cm pieces on an attractive slanted angle. Bring the stock to the boil, season with salt, and blanch the asparagus for around 3–4 minutes, until just tender. Remove with a slotted spoon and spread out over a tray to cool quickly so they keep their bright green colour. Leave the stock in the pan and keep it at a gentle simmer.

Finely slice the white and pale green parts of the spring onions. Melt the butter in a wide pan. Add the spring onions and a pinch of salt and fry gently for around 5 minutes, until softened. Add the very finely chopped garlic and soften for another couple of minutes.

Add the rice to the pot and cook for a couple of minutes, until translucent. Pour in the wine, increase the heat and let it bubble up. When the wine has all been absorbed, start adding the stock in the normal risotto way, keeping it at a moderate bubble and stirring frequently, adding the stock when the last has been absorbed. Aim to keep the risotto loose and mobile but not sodden. After around 15–20 minutes the rice should be cooked – tender and pleasant to eat but still with a slight bite. Depending on your rice, you may not need all the stock.

Take the pan off the heat and stir in the blanched asparagus and Parmesan. Let it sit for a couple of minutes, then loosen with a final ladle of stock if it needs it. Aim for a relaxed creamy finish. Season with salt and pepper as you like it.

Divide the risotto between shallow bowls and spoon the bright green herb oil around to form a moat.

Freshwater Crayfish

Since the 1960s the American signal crayfish has supplanted smaller species of crayfish in many of the shallower, fast-flowing chalk or limestone rivers. They are predators of small fish, consumers of fish eggs, prolific breeders and bank burrowers and they have prospered at the expense of native fish stocks and crayfish.

Native species of crayfish are protected and it is illegal to catch and eat them. But you are unlikely to find the two species co-existing and it's easy to tell the difference. The American signal crayfish is much larger, with claws that are reddish-brown on the underside, while the natives are smaller with paler yellow/white claws. There is plenty of explanatory information on the web to show the difference.

Catching them yourself is an economic approach, since you need at least 500g per person for a meal. In Britain a licence is needed from the Environment Agency, but it is free, easy and quick to obtain. You need an authorized trap (see page 334 for supplier) and the landowner's permission. Once caught they should be left to fast for 2 days or so in fresh water. Any large vessel will do. Chicken wire should be fitted over the top to stop them escaping. Change the water regularly to ensure they have enough oxygen. Or use an outdoor vessel with a constant flow of water running through from a hosepipe.

Alternatively live crayfish can be ordered from a good fishmonger. Keep them in the fridge to lull them while you prepare. Use rubber gloves when handling, picking them up on their back to avoid flaring claws. If you've bought them, give them a dunk and sluice in fresh, cold water before dropping into the boiling cooking pot, as you would lobster or crab.

Most of the flesh is in the tail, with a little in the claws of the large males. To eat, separate the head from the tail and discard. Break open the spiny tail on the underside and peel out the tail flesh. Find the black digestive tract that runs along the tail and remove. The claws are cracked like crab or lobster and tiny, delicate thorns of flesh can be extracted. The shells can be used for fish stock. Crayfish have a delicate flavour and juicy, tender flesh.

Crayfish with Wild Garlic Butter & Lovage Vodka

SERVES 6

The crayfish in broth
3kg live freshwater crayfish
5 litres water
½ a bottle of white wine
3 leeks or onions, sliced
3 sticks of celery, sliced
3 bay leaves
small bunches of fresh mint,
    parsley and dill
1 teaspoon each fennel seeds
    and black peppercorns
5 tablespoons sea salt
1 tablespoon sugar

To serve
lemon wedges, dill fronds
    and crusty bread
wild garlic butter (see below)
lovage shots (see below)

Following the Scandinavian practice of eating quantities of crayfish washed down with aquavit, here is a herby alternative. Make the lovage vodka ahead.

Lovage is a delicious, under-used herb with earthy, aromatic (and even curry-ish) celery flavours. It's not often found in supermarkets but it is easy to grow, shooting up every spring and threatening to take over the garden. If you have difficulty finding lovage, use a small bunch of dill.

Wild garlic butter is also delicious stirred into a risotto, mixed into pasta, or on grilled meat or fish. Substitute an aïoli, in need.

In a large pot, make a stock by combining all the ingredients except the crayfish (reserving some dill fronds) and simmer for around half an hour. Strain the broth and return the liquid to the pot. Bring to a vigorous boil, then add half the crayfish and simmer for 7 minutes. Lift them out with a strainer into a bowl of icy water to stop them cooking. Repeat with the remaining crayfish. Let the stock cool completely, then pour over the strained crayfish and leave them in the fridge for several hours or overnight to soak up the flavoursome broth.

Strain the crayfish and serve at room temperature with the reserved fronds of dill and lemon wedges. Gently heat the wild garlic butter until melted and warm. Pour the butter into little bowls for dipping and the lovage vodka or gin into chilled shot glasses. Crusty bread is essential to mop up the juices.

Lovage Vodka
Pour 500ml of vodka into a jar, add a handful of lovage, making sure it's submerged, then close the jar and leave at room temperature for 2 days. Remove the lovage, decant into a bottle and chill in the fridge or freezer.

Wild Garlic Butter
Mash 100g of very, very finely chopped wild garlic with 250g of butter until well combined. Add salt to taste. Press the butter into a dish, cover well with clingfilm and leave to chill in the fridge or freezer.

GATHER COOK FEAST

Trout with Brown Butter, Fennel & Sorrel

SERVES 2

1 smallish leek, white and pale
    green parts only, finely sliced
    into half-moons
1 medium bulb of fennel,
    trimmed, quartered, cored and
    finely sliced, fronds reserved
80g butter
olive oil
sea salt and black pepper
100ml white wine
around 300g new potatoes, gently
    scrubbed but not peeled
juice of ½ a lemon
2 trout fillets, scaled and pin-boned
    (around 300–350g)
1 bunch of sorrel (around 40g),
    stalks removed and leaves
    sliced into ribbons

The winning combination of delicate fish with brown butter and lemony vegetables will soothe a post-work energy gap. Find delicious new potatoes such as Jersey Royals, pale under muddy coats, fresh from the field, to go alongside.

Soften the leek and fennel in half the butter with a dash of olive oil and a generous pinch of salt until just shy of tender. Add the wine, then reduce the heat and simmer for another 10 minutes, until the vegetables are soft and the wine has evaporated. Check the seasoning and keep warm.

Boil the potatoes, then drain and partially crush each with the back of a wooden spoon. Keep them warm.

In another small pan melt the remaining butter, then continue cooking until the milk solids turn nut brown and it smells of caramel. Add the lemon juice (it will sizzle and spit), swirl to combine and set aside.

Trim the trout fillets as needed and cut each into two neat pieces. Season them with salt and pepper.

Heat a dash of oil in a wide frying pan, preferably non-stick, until shimmering. Add the fish carefully, flesh side down, and fry for a couple of minutes over a high heat. Carefully flip them over and fry on the skin side for another couple of minutes, until the fish is just cooked through and the skin is starting to crisp – aim for a cooked-looking, opaque surface and just a hint of a juicy, slightly translucent centre. Remove the pan from the heat.

Stir the sliced sorrel into the warm fennel mixture and let it wilt. Divide between plates, arrange the potatoes nestled around and stack the fish on top. Give the brown butter a stir and spoon it over the fish and potatoes. Garnish with the reserved fennel fronds.

Hot-smoked Trout

70g fine sea salt

40g white sugar

around 4 teaspoons vodka

4 very fresh trout fillets,
    scaled and pin-boned, skin
    left on (around 600–700g)

around 2–3 tablespoons oak
    sawdust, for smoking

oil, for greasing

Smoky, sticky, brown or rainbow trout is a lunch for any day. Serve with either pressed parsley potatoes (see page 39), or simply boiled new potatoes.

For more detailed information on hot-smoking and how to do it without special equipment, see pages 226–7.

Mix together the salt, sugar and vodka to make a wet paste. Rub gently all over the trout fillets and leave at cool room temperature to lightly cure for 30–45 minutes (don't leave for longer or the fish will become too firm). Carefully brush the majority of the cure off the trout with kitchen paper.

Set up your stove-top smoker with the wood dust on a sheet of foil in the base and place over a low heat. Lightly grease the rack in the smoker. When smoke starts to appear, lay the trout fillets on the rack, skin side down. Cover and cook over a low heat until the fish is just cooked through, about 10 minutes. It's nice if the fillets are still a tad rare in the very centre and just beginning to go smoky sticky brown at the edges.

Serve hot or at room temperature, but best freshly smoked.

Pressed Parsley Potatoes

500g larger Charlotte
    potatoes, peeled

½ a medium red onion, peeled
    and finely sliced

3 cloves of garlic, peeled and
    very finely sliced

2 tablespoons white wine vinegar

30g salted butter

40g fresh flat-leaf parsley,
    stalks removed

sea salt and black pepper

Inspired by a pressed potato and caper recipe in the unparalleled *Nose to Tail Eating* by Fergus Henderson, here is a parsley and vinegar-slaked version to accompany the gin-cured mackerel (see page 95) or the hot-smoked trout (see page 36), or many other fish dishes – especially more sturdy, oily fish.

I have an unapologetic devotion to Charlotte potatoes, which are easily the tastiest waxy potato. Look for bigger examples to avoid a fiddly process, or substitute Nicola or Cara at a push. The waxy texture also helps keep this whole potato loaf together.

You have to plan ahead with this one, making it the day before to meld the flavours and firm the loaf.

Boil the potatoes until properly soft, drain them, put them back into the still-warm pan to dry off, then slice them lengthways as finely as possible (around 2mm thick).

Steam the onion and garlic over boiling water (or over the boiling potatoes, if easy) for around 5–10 minutes until soft and tender. Put them into a small bowl, add the vinegar and leave to steep for 10 minutes or so.

While the potatoes are cooking, melt the butter and line a medium loaf tin with clingfilm, ensuring you have some extra at the sides to fold over the top. Chop the parsley very finely, sprinkling it with some crunchy sea salt and pepper as you chop to help release moisture. Remove the onion and garlic from their bath and squeeze out all the surplus vinegar.

To assemble the pressed potatoes, first cover the base of the loaf tin with a layer of potatoes, add a further grinding of sea salt and pepper, then add a dribble of melted butter, then a layer of chopped parsley and a strewing of onion mix. Repeat until you have used up all the ingredients, finishing with a layer of potato. It should make 3–4 full layers. Fold over the clingfilm to cover and put a second loaf tin inside to press down on the mixture. Place the heaviest weight you can find inside the top tin. Leave in the fridge overnight to firm up and combine flavours.

When you are ready to eat, turn out on to a board, unwrap, season and slice a section per person.

Herbed Rice with Saffron Pike-Perch

SERVES 6

450g basmati rice

2kg broad beans, podded

1 large bunch (around 40g)
    each of fresh coriander, dill,
    chives and chervil

2 very large bunches (around
    80g each) of fresh parsley
    and wild garlic leaves

150g good sea-salted butter

a good pinch of saffron threads

sea salt and black pepper

1kg pike-perch fillets, skinned,
    pin-boned by your fishmonger
    and divided into 12 portions

olive oil

a lemon or two, cut into wedges

MARCH TO MAY FOR WILD GARLIC

An ancient connection of food to changing season survives only in pockets now in our busy lives. The egg and hot cross bun at Easter, the feast at Christmas, pancakes before the start of Lent and the harvest supper are markers for religious festivals, but likely grafted on to pre-Christian celebrations of seasonal change. The spring equinox in Iran marks the first day of the Persian New Year and it is on this day that an Iranian family will often eat *sabzi polo mahi*, a communal rice dish piled high with fresh herbs and eaten with fish.

This is a proposal to join them – to gather generous handfuls of wild garlic and herbs in celebration of the surge of new growth. You may be alarmed at the quantity of herbs, but I urge you to go with it – the herbs soften the buttery rice and infuse it with flavour. The steaming method of cooking the rice creates crunchy shards of golden rice (an Iranian friend called this *dig* – from *tahdig*, the Farsi word for the crust formed at the bottom of the pot), and the saffron infuses the fish with delicate flavour.

I suggest pike-perch or even carp, but well-sourced bass or sea bream can be substituted. Wild garlic could be replaced with a bunch of spring onions and a couple of cloves of garlic, all sliced super-fine.

This is a splendid centrepiece for a gathering.

Wash the rice in cold water and drain. Repeat three more times to flush out all the excess starch (this helps the rice to be fluffy with nice separate grains when cooked). Then leave to soak in cold water for an hour while you prepare everything else.

Bring a saucepan of salted water to the boil. In it blanch the beans for 2 minutes, then drain and refresh in ice-cold water immediately to cool them down (this keeps them green). Replace with fresh cold water if needed. When they are completely cold, drain the beans, then pinch one end and slip them out of their rubbery skins.

Finely chop the leaves and tender stems of all the herbs, and mix together. Keep any tough stems for soups or stews.

Drain the rice. Fill a large saucepan (with a lid that fits) with very well salted water – enough to taste too salty. Bring the water to a vigorous boil and cook the rice for exactly 5 minutes, starting the timer from the moment the rice enters the pot. Drain in a colander and let sit for 5 or so minutes to steam dry.

Return the empty pan to the stove, add the butter and melt over a low heat. Pour half of the butter into a cup for use later. Split the pile of herbs in two – one half to use now, setting the other half aside in a bowl for use later. Add one-third of the rice to the pot, then half of the herbs for using now. Do not mix. Repeat with the next third of the rice and the other half of the herbs. Finish with the last third of the rice. Drizzle the reserved melted butter over the top.

Cover the pot with a tea towel, then place the lid firmly on top, folding the corners of the tea towel over the top so that they don't catch fire. Cook over a medium heat for 8 minutes, then place the pot on the very lowest heat you can manage and continue cooking for another 45 minutes.

Meanwhile, toast the saffron threads in a small, dry frying pan over a medium heat for a minute or two, then grind them to a powder in a small mortar and pestle. Mix the saffron with 2 teaspoons of fine sea salt and sprinkle all over the fish. Grind some black pepper over the fish too and rest at room temperature for a while – ideally half an hour, to absorb more flavour.

Gently pat the fish dry with kitchen paper. Heat a dash of olive oil in a wide frying pan (non-stick helps here) until shimmering. Lay the fish in the pan, skinned side up, and colour over a high heat for around 3–4 minutes. Carefully flip on to the other side for a couple of minutes and continue until the fish is just cooked through. Aim for a cooked, opaque surface and just a hint of juicy translucence at the centre.

Mix the reserved herbs from the bowl and the broad beans into the rice and pile it all on to a good wide platter. Scrape up the crispy rice at the bottom of the pot and tuck it into the pile of rice in shards – it's delicious. Arrange the fish on top and serve immediately, with lots of wedges of lemon to squeeze.

Picking Dandelions, Nettles & Wild Garlic

The best dandelions are gathered in the early spring, when the newest leaves appear. If you look very carefully at the rosette, you will find some quite wide leaves with a broad central rib, and others with a narrower rib and more indented leaf. Some plants will be less developed, with a rosette made up of smaller leaves. If you feel these narrower or smaller leaves, they'll be softer and it's these that will make the most delicious salad. If you have a local dandelion patch you can crop them to promote new growth and extend the eating time by some months. A flower pot over the top of a clump will blanch the shoots to spindly paleness; also excellent with the mustardy dressing on page 22.

Always find a clean site away from roads, feet or paws. Nettles are best picked with the assistance of a pair of rubber gloves (for obvious reasons). Sometimes nettles poke their heads up as early as February or March and that's the best time to catch them. Once the plant is more than a foot high it is too late for tender results. Pick the top 6–10cm only. Wild garlic is a simpler foraging proposition. Once you learn how to identify it correctly you will find it helpfully grows in wide carpets with clean, easy-to-pick leaves. Pick the single stems with length and keep them fresh in a jar of water in a cool place. The early first flush of growth is best for recipes where its tenderness will flourish, such as in salads, for pesto, or raw as a chopped dressing. Later on, as the flowers develop, it is better cooked. Try it with mashed potato and ham as a garlicky colcannon.

GATHER COOK FEAST

Burnt Onions &
Wild Garlic Mayonnaise

SERVES 4 AS A SMALL PLATE

8–12 Catalan calçots or baby leeks
    (depending on size)
12 spring onions
1 scant tablespoon olive oil
sea salt and black pepper

The mayonnaise
1 egg yolk, at room temperature
sea salt and black pepper
juice of ½ a lemon
100ml mild olive oil
a handful of wild garlic (or sorrel,
    or 1 clove of normal garlic),
    sliced very finely

MARCH TO MAY FOR WILD GARLIC

There are quite a few varieties of leafy onion (family name allium), variously named – spring onion, green onion, continental onion, scallions or even baby leeks and Catalan calçots – and all will equally lend themselves to this simple small dish, solo, or in combination with each other as here. The caramel tang of soft, slightly charred onion combines with the garlicky sauce in a gratifying way.

The greenish, fresh taste of wild garlic makes a more subtle mayonnaise, but you could also use normal garlic. One clove of ordinary garlic will substitute for the wild garlic, or sorrel would be lovely too – use the same quantity as the wild garlic.

Heat the oven to 220°C/200°C fan/gas 7. Prepare the alliums. Remove any blemished outer leaves and the strands of roots. Make sure you leave the bulb of the root intact to keep each onion or leek together. If using leeks, split them lengthways to ensure you have washed out any grit or earth that may have accumulated between the layers of leaves. Wash the alliums thoroughly and pat dry with a tea towel. Scatter them on a baking tray. Toss with the olive oil and season liberally with salt and pepper. Place in the oven for 15–20 minutes, until charred at the edges. Check after 5–10 minutes and use tongs to turn them over so that they char evenly.

While the alliums are cooking, make the mayonnaise. Put the egg yolk into a bowl together with a pinch of sea salt and a teaspoon of the lemon juice. Start whisking the egg either by hand or with an electric whisk. Then gradually add the oil, drop by scarce drop. Keep going, ensuring your mixture is thickening well. Once this is happening you can increase the flow of the oil. When you have a smooth firm mayonnaise, add the remaining lemon juice, which will slacken the mixture. It should not be stiff. Take the very finely sliced wild garlic leaves, sprinkle some salt over, and re-chop, this way and that, to make a bruised paste. Add this paste to the mayonnaise, then check the seasoning and add more salt, pepper or lemon to your taste.

When cooked, remove the alliums from the oven, arrange on a plate and serve with the wild garlic mayonnaise.

Wild Weed Pasties

SERVES 4

1 tablespoon olive oil

2 round shallots or 1 banana
  shallot, peeled and thinly sliced

2 cloves of garlic, peeled
  and finely chopped

250g dandelion or other leaves,
  carefully washed, spun but not
  dry, trimmed and chopped

60g raisins, soaked
  in a little warm water

150g Feta, crumbled

a few fresh parsley leaves, chopped

50g capers, drained of brine
  and chopped

1 egg, beaten

2 tablespoons yoghurt

50g pine nuts, toasted

sea salt and black pepper

a little freshly grated nutmeg

a packet of filo pastry

80g butter, melted

FEBRUARY TO MAY FOR
YOUNG WEEDS

I made these pasties on holiday on the sun-baked island of Lefkada in the Ionian islands of Greece. I bought a couple of very large bunches of very muddy weeds – there called *horta*, a catch-all name for weeds of an edible nature – and cooked these little pasties to eat on the beach.

Patience Gray writes with lyricism about the eating of weeds in her wonderful book *Honey from a Weed*. To pick ingredients from the land is grounding and, when gathered carefully, preparation can be simplified. Here I have chosen dandelions to substitute for *horta*. Dandelions can be mixed with other foraged spring leaves – Good King Henry, nettles, hogweed, fat hen or sorrel are good ones to start with – or substitute sorrel, rocket or spinach, alone or in combination, for a non-foraged version (see page 337 for foraging info). In Greece I made my own filo pastry, but shop-bought is a good deal easier.

In a large, lidded frying pan, heat the olive oil and soften the shallots and garlic over a low heat until transparent and beginning to turn a little golden (about 10 minutes or so). Add the drained but still-moist leaves and sweat with the lid on until soft and tender (3–5 minutes depending on the tenderness of the leaves). Remove from the heat and cool.

Drain the raisins and add, together with the crumbled Feta, parsley, capers, egg, yoghurt and pine nuts. Season to taste with salt, pepper and grated nutmeg.

Heat the oven to 200°C/180°C fan/gas 6.

To assemble, take a sheet of filo pastry and brush it all over with melted butter, then fold lengthways into three, sealing the butter under the two folds. Put a tablespoon of dandelion mixture on the bottom edge of the strip. Now begins the origami – fold the bottom edge of the strip to the left-hand edge to form a triangle. Continue folding and folding from one edge to the other, while retaining the triangle shape. Use a little water to seal the final edge to the surface of the pasty. Brush with melted butter and lay on a lined baking tray. Continue in this way until all the pasties are assembled.

Bake in the oven until golden brown – about 30–40 minutes.

Two Ways with Spring Pasta

SERVES 4

For wild garlic pesto spaghetti
60g walnut pieces
125g wild garlic leaves, washed
    well and spun dry
60g Parmesan, in small cubes,
    and more to grate over
100ml olive oil
sea salt and black pepper
the juice of up to ½ a lemon
360–400g good-quality spaghetti

For bitter green orecchiette
sea salt and black pepper
400g bitter greens, ends of stalks
    removed, tough hollow stems
    discarded, rinsed and spun dry,
    rest of stalks finely chopped
2 red chillies, deseeded and
    very finely chopped
2 cloves of garlic, peeled and
    very finely chopped
6 anchovy fillets, very finely chopped
2 tablespoons olive oil
360–400g orecchiette
80g Parmesan, finely grated

MARCH TO MAY FOR WILD
GARLIC, JANUARY TO APRIL
FOR CIME DI RAPA

Here are two options for a springtime pasta urge – the first sweetly nutty and garlicky, the second a hunger-quenching salty/bitter option.

Wild Garlic Pesto Spaghetti

Once the wild garlic starts poking its head up from the soil I head to the river to fill baskets from the thick carpets of 'ramps' growing alongside, returning week after week until the season is done. Wild garlic (*Allium ursinum* or ramsons, ramps, buckrams, wood or bear garlic) is, with practice, an easily recognizable plant, pushing up its perfect, soft, spear-like leaves in clumps or carpets on verges in woods or damp spots between March and May. Wild garlic is native to the British Isles and its presence, along with bluebells, is a faint echo of long-vanished ancient woodlands. (See page 337 for foraging guides.)

This recipe is now a widely adopted forager's classic and it's super-easy. Other nuts can be used for variety – almonds, hazelnuts and even sweet chestnuts.

Toast the walnuts in a dry pan until they begin to give off their nutty fragrance and colour a little in places. Do not over-toast because it will make the pesto bitter.

Put the leaves, the nuts and the cubes of Parmesan into a food processor and whizz at full speed to combine. Then pour in the olive oil until a thick paste is formed. Use the spatula a few times to drag the edges down into the centre to ensure an even blend. Finally season with salt and pepper and a very little lemon juice to taste.

Cook the spaghetti to al dente bite and stir through a good generous slick of pesto. Pile on to a warm plate and grate over a little Parmesan.

Bitter Green Orecchiette

The season for cime di rapa (also called turnip tops, rapini or broccoli rabe) is longer, from the beginning of January to April. The best come from Puglia but are also available here later in the season. For the adventurous, foraged cleavers tops, picked at the very beginning of the growing season in March, are a good wild substitute, but be sure to correctly identify.

Fill a pan with plenty of cold water, add salt and bring to the boil. Add the prepared greens and boil until soft – start with the stems, cook for 4 minutes, then add the leaves and cook for a further 2 minutes. Then drain, but save a mug of the cooking water for later. Chop the drained greens roughly and plunge them into cold water to keep them green while you cook the rest of the ingredients.

Cook the pasta to al dente in plenty of salted water.

Soften the chillies, garlic and anchovies in the olive oil over a medium heat until they are softly combined and melted together.

Add the chopped greens and a couple of tablespoons of the cooking water and cook for a few more minutes until the flavours have combined.

Toss the sauce with the cooked pasta, season with salt and pepper to taste and add the Parmesan to finish.

Duck in a Pot
with Spring Vegetables

SERVES 6–8

1 farmed (or 2 wild) duck,
    weighing 2–2.5kg, with giblets
sea salt and black pepper
2 litres good chicken stock
2 leeks with green leaves, washed
1 large or 2 small fennel bulbs
2 large carrots, peeled and
    roughly chopped
2 sticks of celery, chopped
    into 2 or 3 pieces
several sprigs of fresh thyme
    and parsley
2 bay leaves
12–15 black peppercorns
12–15 coriander seeds
4 cloves
18 baby new potatoes, scrubbed
12 baby carrots, scrubbed
    and topped if needed
6 baby turnips, cut into wedges
12 stems of asparagus, tough base
    removed, chopped into 5cm sticks
12 stems of purple sprouting
    broccoli, tough parts removed
a handful of tiny broad beans
12 red radishes, leaves
    removed, but with 1cm of stalk
    retained for the look of it
a handful of spinach, washed
    and spun dry

On a blustery weekend in April, a pot of rich, flavoursome duck can cook slowly, developing its air of steamy, laundry spring-cleanness and leaving plenty of time for walks before sharing a well-deserved lunch with friends. A wide bowl for each on the table will be filled with tender duck and delicate vegetables, all swimming in fragrant broth, with a zingy, green kick of cornichon and herb sauce alongside.

If buying wild duck, do ask your butcher to make sure the gizzards have been split and cleaned. Wild duck will be smaller and leaner than farmed duck. Expect a wilder taste too; a product of varied herbal and weedy grazing.

Don't discard the duck liver. It can be browned in butter until golden and sliced over some good salad leaves. Deglaze the pan with a dash of vinaigrette dressing and pour over the salad for good rich flavour. Any leftover broth can be used in the same way as chicken stock, and the skimmed fat is wonderful for roasting potatoes. Delicate, fragrant chervil (a flavour cross between tarragon and parsley) is worth the trouble of searching for (see sources at the back of the book).

This is even better reheated on day two.

Season the duck inside and out with salt and leave for an hour to give the seasoning time to penetrate.

Put the duck and its innards (except the liver – see above) into a large pot and pour over the chicken stock, then top up with cold water until the duck is submerged.

Remove the green tops and tough outer layers of the leeks as well as the stalks, base and fat outer layer of the fennel. Roughly chop these trimmings and add to the stock, together with the chopped carrots and celery, thyme, parsley, bay and spices. Chop the remaining white parts of the leeks into fat logs and split the fennel into wedges and keep these to add as finishing vegetables at the end.

Bring the pot to the boil, skimming off the scum periodically, then let the duck simmer gently in its aromatic bath for around 1½–1¾ hours, until the meat is very tender. Turn the duck over once or twice so that it cooks evenly.

The herb sauce
10–15 cornichons
a small bunch each of fresh chervil,
    chives, tarragon and parsley
olive oil
1 tablespoon smooth Dijon mustard
1 teaspoon red wine vinegar

WILD DUCK SEASON – SEPTEMBER
TO END JANUARY, FARMED DUCK –
AVAILABLE ALL YEAR

For the sauce, whizz the cornichons and herbs together until finely chopped, then add olive oil to make a loose paste. Stir in mustard, vinegar and salt to taste.

Remove the duck from the pot and when cool pull off large pieces of skinless meat and put them into an ovenproof serving dish. Strain the duck's cooking liquid into a separate pot. Let the fat rise to the top and then skim it off (see above for uses). Pour enough of the strained broth over to almost cover the duck, seal with foil and keep warm in a low oven.

Pour the remaining broth back into the pot and boil hard, uncovered, to reduce for 5 minutes or so. Then taste and season with sea salt and black pepper. Now sequentially cook the serving vegetables in the broth, adjusting each of their cooking times to their size and type. Aim to have a bowlful of perfectly cooked bright veggies at the end.

Start with baby potatoes, carrots and turnips. Cook for 10 minutes or so, until they are just becoming tender on the outside. Then add the fennel and leeks saved from the stock-making and cook for a further 5 minutes. Next add the asparagus, broccoli, broad beans and radishes. After a minute or so more, add a handful of spinach to wilt on the top.

Arrange the cooked vegetables, generous ladles of the broth and the duck in shallow bowls and serve with the herb sauce alongside. Make sure everyone has a radish or two and a slick of spinach to give definition to the plate.

GATHER COOK FEAST

Duck Breasts
with Spinach

SERVES 4

3–4 duck breasts
  (you'll need 650–700g)
sea salt and black pepper
¾ teaspoon five-spice powder
4 cloves of garlic, peeled
  and finely sliced
4cm piece of ginger, peeled and
  cut into tiny matchsticks
2 hot red chillies, deseeded and
  finely sliced
700g spinach leaves, tough stems
  removed, washed well

The sauce
5 teaspoons light soy sauce
2 teaspoons dark soy sauce
2 teaspoons cornflour
2 tablespoons Shaoxing
  Chinese rice wine
1 tablespoon sesame oil
2 teaspoons soft light brown sugar
8 tablespoons water

Fat, succulent duck breasts love Chinese flavours. Slice these glistening dark breasts over bright green spinach and serve them with a pile of warm, soft rice or wheat noodles. Most people find a whole duck breast more than enough – and duck breasts vary so much in size – so follow the weight required and use your judgement when shopping, rather than following a one-per-person stricture.

It may seem a bore, but resting is important – twice here, after the browning stage and after the oven. This allows the muscle fibres to relax. Taking time to do this will give you a much more tender and juicy result.

Use a very sharp knife to score the skin of the duck breasts in a fine criss-cross pattern, cutting into the layer of fat under the skin but not as far as the flesh. Season the breasts all over with salt, pepper and five-spice powder and massage gently. Leave at room temperature for around 45 minutes, to allow time for the seasoning to penetrate.

Meanwhile make the sauce, by combining the soy sauces and cornflour to make a wet slurry and then stirring in all the other ingredients.

Place the duck breasts skin side down in a wide frying pan (the biggest you have, to contain all the spinach you'll be cooking later) and set over a very low heat for around 15 minutes – to render out the fat and crisp up the skin, but not cook the flesh; the breasts should remain very rare. As the fat accumulates in the pan, pour it out into a small container (good for roasting potatoes – freeze for later). Remove the breasts to a baking tray, skin side up, and let rest for 15 minutes. This step can be done in advance, but don't wash up the pan just yet.

Heat the oven to 220°C/200°C fan/gas 7.

To finish cooking the breasts, roast them in the oven for around 6 minutes until medium rare. Then bring the breasts out of the oven and rest them on the roasting tin, loosely tented with foil, for 5–10 minutes, while you cook the spinach.

Heat the pan again with around 1 tablespoon of duck fat in it. Add the garlic, ginger and chillies and cook for a couple of minutes, stirring to loosen. Add the spinach and toss to coat with the aromatic flavours. If room is limited in your pan, turn the spinach with a pair of tongs or a couple of forks to assist wilting: as the bottom layer wilts, pop some more in at the top and turn until it has all gone slack and glossy. As soon as the spinach has wilted, give the sauce a stir, pour it in and let it bubble up and thicken. Add any juices that have come out of the duck.

Slice the duck breasts on an angle against the grain of the meat. Make a bed of the glossy spinach, and arrange the slices of duck breast over, then pour around the remaining sauce from the pan. If you like, add some rice or noodles on the side.

Rhubarb & Blood Oranges

SERVES 4–6

300–400g forced rhubarb, with
    base and leaves removed
70g caster sugar, plus a little more
2 medium unwaxed blood oranges,
    washed and dried
thick double cream

JANUARY TO APRIL FOR EARLY,
PINK FORCED RHUBARB, DECEMBER
TO MARCH FOR BLOOD ORANGES

The season for these two ingredients helpfully coincides from January to March, with the appearance of the first pale pink forced rhubarb and the last intensely red blood oranges. The two colours hum prettily together. This is super-simple and a very refreshing end to a meal.

Heat the oven to 220°C/200°C fan/gas 7.

If your rhubarb is tender, all you need do is chop the stems into 4cm pieces. Take a piece of foil big enough to both double over the rhubarb and make a pocket with a good seal, and place it on a baking tray. Arrange the rhubarb in the centre in a single layer, sprinkled with 50g of caster sugar, then fold the foil over the top and crimp the edges to seal.

Now prepare the oranges: slice across each whole orange in rounds (around the equator of the orange, not top to bottom) as finely as you can – 2mm thick is ideal. Remove any pips and discard the ends of the oranges. You will end up with the thinnest cartwheels of orange and rind.

Drape another large piece of foil over a second baking tray and arrange the slices in the centre, overlapping as little as possible. Scatter the remaining 20g of caster sugar over them. Bring up the edges of the foil to make an envelope and crimp the edges together to seal.

Put both baking trays into the oven for 10 minutes.

Take a peek inside the foil after 10 minutes to check if the rhubarb is tender. When it is, remove from the oven and set aside. The oranges will take around 5–8 minutes more to become soft. When they are soft, open up the foil. Scatter a little more sugar over the exposed rings and leave them in the oven to gently caramelize. It should take 5–10 minutes more, but keep a close eye on them so they don't burn. They are done when they begin to take a little colour around the edges and in the thinner parts.

Assemble your plates with the rhubarb in the centre, and with slices of tangy orange balanced against the pile of rhubarb. Pour over any juices from the foil packets. Serve just warm, with good thick double cream.

    GATHER COOK FEAST

Blackcurrant Leaf
Cooked Cream

MAKES 4 SMALL POTS

30 blackcurrant leaves,
    washed and dried
1 vanilla pod, split
50ml full cream milk
450ml double cream
2½ sheets of gelatine
50g caster sugar

APRIL TO MAY FOR TENDER
BLACKCURRANT LEAVES

The fragrance and taste of blackcurrant leaves are surprising in their delicate intensity, a mysterious aroma of blackcurrants in greener, more leafy form. Here they are infused overnight to gently draw out their flavour into the creaminess.

In a good spring, blackcurrants start sprouting small leaves in April and you can carry on using them until the end of May. They tend to lose their flavour somewhat once the bush is putting effort into berry production.

If you aren't lucky enough to have a bush in your garden, find a friend who has one and beg a few leaves. It will be a revelation.

This cooked cream will have a soft set. Serve at room temperature.

Crumple the washed and dried blackcurrant leaves and place with the vanilla pod in a snap-top plastic box or such with the milk and cream. Leave overnight in the fridge to infuse.

The next day, empty into a pan over a medium heat and warm through, until just short of boiling.

Soak the gelatine according to the packet instructions.

Remove the milk pan from the heat and sieve out the leaves, squishing all the cream back into the pan. Fish around to find the vanilla pod. Scrape the black seeds from the pod into the cream mixture. Add the sugar and warm the mixture through until the sugar has dissolved. Remove from the heat.

Squeeze the sheets of gelatine to express most of the water and add to the hot milk. Stir gently but well, to ensure the gelatine is effectively distributed and has dissolved completely. Pour the mixture into four small pots, ramekins or little cups or glasses.

Cool to room temperature, then place in the fridge until set.

Lenten Almond Biscuits

MAKES 10–12 SMALL FINGERS

½ a vanilla pod
100g plain flour
60g ground almonds
50g caster sugar
100g salted butter,
    at room temperature
a couple of drops of almond extract
30g flaked almonds, toasted

The almond is a magical ingredient. The purest shape – like a perfectly manicured nail – they infuse pastries and cakes with a deep, gratifying meaty chewiness. Such is the nourishing satisfaction delivered by this pale and magnificent nut, elaborate confections were made from almonds to substitute for meat during the Lenten fast in medieval times – the origin of the word 'sweetmeat'.

Eat these little biscuits with ice cream, some berries, or on their own.

Heat the oven to 190°C/170°C fan/gas 5.

Split the vanilla pod along its length and scrape out the seeds with the blade of the knife. Keep the empty pod to flavour caster sugar.

Make a pile of the flour, ground almonds and caster sugar in a bowl or on a clean board. Place the butter and the vanilla seeds in the centre and add the almond extract. Then, using your hands, squeeze the ingredients together, mushing the body of the flours into the butter, until you have a well-mixed and textured dough ball. Once combined, squash the flaked almonds into the mixture until well distributed.

Take a piece of baking parchment large enough to fit one of your baking trays and put it on a flat surface for rolling. Place the ball of dough in the centre of the parchment and, using a rolling pin, roll out the dough into a neat rectangle. You will find the edges break and crack, but don't worry, just firm them up with your fingers. The finished dough should be a good 1cm deep. Slide the paper carefully on to your baking tray. Then score through the dough with a sharp knife to make rough fingers.

Put the baking tray into the oven for 20–25 minutes, until the biscuits are just starting to colour at the edges. Remove the tray and allow to cool. Your section markers will have blurred in the cooking, so now cut the fingers again with a sharp knife.

If you can, leave until absolutely cold before eating.

Vin d'Épine

MAKES NEARLY 1 LITRE

1 bottle of good-quality rosé wine
175ml vodka or grappa
100g white granulated sugar
   (or rose sugar as a variation)
50g young blackthorn shoots
   (see note on the right), washed
   and spun dry

APRIL TO MAY FOR
BLACKTHORN SHOOTS

The tender, ruddy-tinted shoots of the blackthorn bush start growing in April or May – depending on the year. Be sure to identify the bushes (using a trusted reference book) the previous autumn, when they bear the familiar black bloomed sloe berries, or in the spring, when the blackthorn is the first in the hedgerow to bear white blossom. It may be hard to tell one from another when largely bare-branched (although the sharp thorns are a giveaway). You'll need to pick a salad spinner or colander-full because the tips are light, but weigh the gleanings to get the right amount. Each tip will smell remarkably like bitter almonds. This is because the leaves, berries and flowers contain the cyanogenic glycocides associated with that telltale smell. But, drunk in moderation, this is not a risk – hordes of sloe gin drinkers, apricot or wild plum eaters and almond extract cake-cookers have survived with no ill effects and all these contain the same compounds. Pick 10–15cm of the supple tip of the shoots, including the clusters of leaves attached to it. Pick a few from each branch – don't strip the whole bush.

Anna carefully researched and developed this wonderful recipe from the French classic, using rosé and vodka to infuse the delicious almond/plum flavour of the shoots. The result is a very pretty pink drink, which makes a really delicious springtime aperitif served in tumblers with a very little sparkling water, ice and a twist of lemon or orange zest. We both now make this in quantity each spring. It's so lovely.

Combine all the ingredients in a 1 litre jar, making sure the shoots are fully submerged. Seal and leave somewhere out of direct sunshine for up to 3 weeks, until it smells strongly of almonds and plums. You can give the jar the odd gentle shake to encourage the sugar to dissolve.

Strain the wine through a sieve lined with a piece of damp muslin or other fine cloth. Press down on the leaves to extract as much wine as possible. Pour the strained wine into sterilized bottles (see page 105 for instructions) and store in the fridge, where it will keep happily for several months – but it may not remain there that long.

Serve in small tumblers over ice with a twist of orange or lemon zest and with or without a little dilution of fizzy water.

GATHER COOK FEAST

FRESH SHARP WAVES
HERRING CLAM
SURGE BRINE PICKLE
SALTWATER CAPER
BREAKER DULSE
PEBBLE MARRAM

CRAB SALTMARSH
SAFFRON SAMPHIRE
SHELLS LEMON
LITTORAL SANDBANK

One Easter, I camped with my soon-to-be-husband, Jamie, and a good friend, Monica, on the clifftop overlooking a long sandy beach in Pembrokeshire. We weren't really allowed to be there, but we hid our tiny tent in a hollow and hunkered down. We swam too, and by the end of the day I had such a strong need to eat something from the sea I can still remember it now, many years later. I don't remember what we actually ate; we were young and poor and vegetarian, so fish was not an option anyway. But I remember I dreamed of seaweed.

Seaweed is so packed full of minerals and vitamins it makes any dish that contains it uniquely satisfying. In Japan, China and Korea it is grown on ropes and nets, an aquaculture that helps reduce fishing pressure and improves economic conditions and nutrition. Could seaweed be grown in this way around our coasts if we decided we liked it more? It's an interesting idea. Laverbread has long been a foraged staple in my home county of Carmarthenshire, eaten for breakfast with bacon.

When compiling the recipes for this section the depleted state of our coastal waters was very much at front of mind. But the situation is changing all the time. What may be plentiful this week may be fished out next year. The responsible cook should keep up to date on states of fish stocks and buy from sustainable sources wherever possible. Look for fish that have been caught using lower-impact methods – inshore boats, hook and line, jigs, pots or creels. There is plenty of information available online (see Further Reading & Learning on page 337).

This section isn't all about fish – the salt marshes of the Welsh littoral provide delicious lamb with a sweet and distinct salty savour. There are foraged ingredients to try too – the lime-green stems of alexanders to braise and butter; sea buckthorn berries in a classic burnt cream. And finally – salted ice creams.

Raw Rhubarb, Cucumber
& Radish Salad

SERVES 4 AS A SMALL PLATE

250g cucumber (half a big
    one or 2 mini ones), sliced
    into curls with a peeler
200g slender, pink rhubarb stems
    (around 2 stems), trimmed and
    chopped into tiny rough shards
1½ teaspoons fine sea salt
200g red radishes (8–10),
    sliced into fine rounds
1½ tablespoons lemon juice
leaves from 4 sprigs of fresh mint

APRIL TO JUNE FOR
FIELD RHUBARB

This sounds stranger than it is in actuality. In a miraculous way, the salt diminishes the tartness of the rhubarb and confirms it as a stunning salad ingredient. Put a sizzling, sea-fresh, grilled mackerel alongside and I will join you for an early summer lunch.

Place the sliced cucumber and rhubarb in a colander and sprinkle with the salt. Toss gently to distribute the salt, then balance over a bowl to drip for 20–30 minutes.

Rinse the cucumber and rhubarb swiftly under a running tap, then drain and dry with kitchen paper. Place in a wide bowl along with the fine rounds of radish. Sprinkle over the lemon juice and let it sit while you prepare the mint.

Stack the mint leaves in two neat piles. Take one and roll it up into a fat cigar. Using a very sharp knife cut across the cigar to create fine ribbons. Repeat with the other pile of mint leaves and add all the mint to the salad. Gently lift and mix everything together and serve without too much delay.

French Breakfast Radishes with Anchovy Aïoli

SERVES 4

Eat crunchy, new season French Breakfast radishes dipped alternately in flaky sea salt and anchovy aïoli with a drink while waiting for supper.

Wash 16–20 radishes, then cut off the tops, leaving around 2cm of stem.

Put 1 egg yolk into a bowl together with a pinch of sea salt and a teaspoon of lemon juice. Start whisking the egg either by hand or with an electric whisk. Then gradually add some olive oil, drop by scarce drop. Keep adding oil in tiny drops until the mixture has started to thicken – once this happens you can increase the flow of oil to a dribble until the mayonnaise is smooth and thick. Then stir in 1 teaspoon more of lemon juice, 2–3 mashed anchovies, 1 crushed clove of garlic and 1 tablespoon of crème fraîche, and season with sea salt and black pepper.

Serve the radishes on a plate with a pile of flaky sea salt and a small pot of aïoli for dipping.

LATE SPRING OR EARLY SUMMER
FOR NEW RADISHES

Dressed Crab, Broad Bean
& Asparagus Salad

SERVES 2 FOR LUNCH

1 dressed crab – brown and white meat

2 tablespoons crème fraîche

sea salt and black pepper

a good squeeze of lemon juice

½ red chilli, deseeded
    and finely chopped

2 spring onions, the white and pale
    green parts, very finely sliced

zest of 1 lemon

250g asparagus

250g broad beans, podded

6 leaves of butter lettuce, washed,
    dried and perfect

The dressing

a small bunch of mixed soft,
    fresh herbs – for example
    parsley, tarragon, mint, chives,
    finely chopped

2 tablespoons olive oil

1 tablespoon lemon juice

sea salt and black pepper

APRIL TO NOVEMBER FOR CRAB,
APRIL TO JUNE FOR ASPARAGUS

Delicious crab is a sustainable catch you can buy with a clear conscience from around the rocky shores of the British Isles.

Dressed crab is prepared as a way to present both the white and brown meat in the crab shell. It makes life easy for the cook, who only has to scoop out the delicious flesh (checking for small pieces of shell) and combine with asparagus, butter lettuce and broad beans.

After years of being a broad-bean-skinning-denier, I am now a convert. It doesn't take long and the end result is both prettier and more delicious. You can use a wide variety of herbs to accent this meal – as well as those below, try lemon balm, sweet cicely, salad burnet or dill.

First, scoop out the crabmeat and mix together with the crème fraîche, a little sea salt and black pepper and a good squeeze of lemon juice, the chilli, spring onions and lemon zest.

Next mix the chopped herbs with the rest of the dressing ingredients and season with salt and pepper.

The vigorous tenderness of asparagus can be spoilt by a hard, stringy end, but there is a neat trick to keep the entire stalk equally succulent. If you bend the stem gently but firmly, feeling for the point of weakness, the stem will snap at precisely the spot where stringy meets tender. The discarded base ends need not be thrown away but can serve to enhance stock for an asparagus-friendly dish, so keep them for later.

Now cook the beans and asparagus. Find a pot big enough to hold the asparagus at an angle (mine is an 18cm one with a lid). Fill with 5cm of salted water and bring to the boil. Add the broad beans to the pan and boil them for around 2–3 minutes. Fish out the cooked beans with a slotted spoon and plunge them into a bowl of iced water to preserve their bright green colour.

When cool, pinch the end of each bean to make a small opening, then squeeze the other end to express the inner bean.

While you are peeling the beans, the asparagus can be cooking. Prop the asparagus in the same pan – with the base of the stems simmering

DRESSED CRAB, BROAD BEAN &
ASPARAGUS SALAD / CONTINUED

in a few centimetres of water and the tips cooking in the steam – for
around 4–5 minutes, until just tender. Drain and cool.

Arrange the leaves of butter lettuce, a good scoop of crabmeat,
the asparagus and the broad beans on a plate and dribble the herb
mixture over all.

Saffron
Fish Stew

SERVES 4 HEARTY EATERS

1 large onion, peeled and chopped

2 tablespoons olive oil

1 large clove of garlic, peeled
   and finely chopped

500ml white wine

3 sticks of celery, chopped

1 carrot, peeled and finely chopped

1 medium to large potato, peeled
   and finely chopped

1 head of fennel, trimmed and chopped

1 leek, trimmed and sliced into rings

sea salt and black pepper

1 tied bunch of fresh parsley, thyme
   and a bay leaf

1 lightly packed teaspoon
   saffron threads

1 litre fish stock

350g cod fillet, skinned, cubed

250g hake fillet, skinned, cubed

10 scallops, halved, coral separated

350ml cream

10 large (raw or cooked) prawns,
   in their shells

a handful of chopped fresh
   parsley leaves

The first saffron fish stew I tasted was on an island called Sandhamn in the bleak, outer reaches of the Stockholm archipelago. Arriving tired, grubby and hungry after an extended sail, we washed and brushed up, then climbed an outside staircase to reach a light-filled clapboard harbour restaurant room, sinking gratefully into chairs around a table covered with linen set with silver. Here we enjoyed the most delicious saffron fish stew. This is my version, which recreates, as faithfully as I can, that first memorable taste.

It is easy to make your own fish stock or find a well-made version to buy. You can make this stew with almost any white fish, choosing according to what is good and fresh and well caught.

The stock

Put 1kg of fish carcasses into a large lidded pan together with a few peeled and chopped vegetables – 1 onion, 2 celery sticks, 2 carrots and a leek is ideal. Add a bay leaf and 10 peppercorns and pour in cold water to cover. Put the lid on the pan and bring to the boil, then turn down the heat and continue to simmer for 20 minutes, skimming the froth off the top from time to time. Remove from the heat and strain the liquid for use in the stew. Excess stock can be frozen.

The stew

Over a medium heat soften the onion in the olive oil in a large pan – around 3–5 minutes. Add the garlic and cook for another couple of minutes. Add the wine and boil hard for 5 minutes. Then add all the other vegetables, season well with salt and pepper and give everything a good stir. Lower the heat a little and add the herbs, saffron and fish stock, simmering for around 20 minutes until the vegetables are tender. Meanwhile, season the cod, hake and scallops, and add to the pan once the vegetables are tender. Check to see if the stew is well covered with liquid – if not, add a little more water. Bring to a gentle simmer (gentle so as not to break up the delicate fish) and cook for around 5 minutes, until the fish is nearly tender.

Add the cream and prawns and cook for 2–3 minutes more. Check the seasoning and stir in the parsley. Serve in large bowls, with chunks of good bread.

Laver & Oatmeal Pancakes
with Asparagus & Poached Egg

MAKES 6 SMALL CAKES

20g butter
1 banana shallot, peeled and
    very finely chopped
4 rashers of fine-cut, smoked,
    dry-cured bacon, finely chopped
a small handful of fresh flat-leaf
    parsley leaves, chopped
200g laverbread
100g porridge oats
black pepper
2–3 stems of asparagus per
    person, tough ends removed
1 egg per person

The seaweed *Porphyra umbilicalis* has a better-known relation, *Porphyra yezoensis*, which when dried and toasted is wrapped around sushi and goes by the name of nori. The *umbilicalis* cousin has been prepared in the West Country and Wales for centuries, where it is harvested from the sea, boiled and sold as laverbread. The increase in popularity of Japanese food and our consequent familiarization with the taste of seaweed has now created scope for a wider enjoyment of native seaweeds. You can buy laverbread in tins from specialist stores (see sources, page 335) or, if you are in South Wales, the wonderful Swansea or Carmarthen markets have stalls specializing in cockles and laverbread rolled in oats.

The classic approach is to roll laverbread in oatmeal and cook it with Welsh bacon in the same pan. Here's my version of this.

Take half the butter and melt it in a non-stick pan. Add the shallots and soften, turning constantly for 2–3 minutes. Add the chopped bacon and continue to stir until the bacon releases its fat and the shallots and bacon become a little crispy. Finally, toss in the parsley and stir around until the leaves relax and become darkly green and soft. This will only take a minute or so.

Mix the laverbread, oats and the shallot/bacon/parsley mixture together and form them with your fingers into six or so loose cakes. There is no need to season them with salt, as the sea has already done the job, but add a turn or two of black pepper.

Use the same pan to fry up your laver cakes. Melt the rest of the butter and when it's good and warm, brown the cakes on each side for 3 minutes or so. They should be toasty on each side. Keep the cakes warm while you cook the asparagus and the eggs.

Fill a wide saucepan with a couple of inches of salted water and bring to the boil. Put in the asparagus spears and, a few seconds later, find a space of clear water to slip in the eggs for poaching. Cook gently for 2–3 minutes, then delicately remove from the water using a slotted spoon. Make sure you have wiggled the spoon enough to drain off all the water, then arrange the eggs and asparagus over the laver cakes.

GATHER COOK FEAST

GATHER COOK FEAST

Grilled Octopus
with Lovage & Dill

SERVES 4–6 AS A SMALL PLATE,
2–4 AS A MAIN COURSE

1 octopus (or multiple smaller),
    weighing 1–1.5kg (previously
    frozen), cleaned
2 glasses of white wine (around 320ml)
1 onion, peeled and sliced
4 cloves of garlic, peeled
    and smashed using the
    flat blade of a knife
2 bay leaves
2 teaspoons black peppercorns
1 lemon, sliced
a small bundle of fresh parsley stalks
a small bundle of fresh thyme sprigs
50ml lemon juice
50ml extra virgin olive oil
1 tablespoon very finely
    chopped lovage
1 tablespoon very finely
    chopped fresh dill
sea salt and black pepper
1 lemon, cut into wedges

SUMMER FOR LOVAGE & DILL

In the fading light of a warm early summer evening we grilled pieces of octopus over a fragrant wood barbecue with a glass in hand.

I couldn't imagine you'd choose to tenderize octopus by striking it against coastal rocks or to massage it for some hours with salt, which are the traditional methods. To avoid this trial, order frozen from a good fishmonger and the freezing process will tenderize it. If fresh, make sure you ask the fishmonger to clean it, removing the eyes, beak and guts.

Most octopus is imported from Spain or Portugal, although some are available from Cornwall. As I write, octopus or squid is not subject to quotas – stocks are stable and being monitored. Help it stay that way by choosing to buy pot or jig caught, rather than trawled. The former is a low-impact species-specific catch, the latter is an indiscriminate fishing method that damages the sea-bed and produces a by-catch of wasted sea life – do ask about fishing methods when buying fish.

Put the octopus into a large pot along with the wine, onion, garlic, bay leaves, black peppercorns, sliced lemon, parsley stalks and thyme. Add enough cold water to cover the octopus and bring to a gentle boil. Cover, reduce the heat and simmer very gently for 45–60 minutes, until the octopus is totally tender. Lift it out and let it cool. (The broth can be strained and saved for a seafood risotto or fish stew.)

If large, cut off the octopus's head (it should be easy to see where the head attaches and separate it from the legs) and slice it in half. Divide the octopus into its eight legs and put into a dish with the head. Smaller octopus may be kept whole. Mix the lemon juice, olive oil, lovage and dill and pour over the octopus. Marinate in the fridge for several hours or overnight. Bring out half an hour before grilling.

Light an outdoor charcoal grill or place a cast-iron ridged grill pan over a high heat. You need a really high heat to char the octopus in order to develop the smoky, grilled flavour. Season the pieces well with salt and pepper and make sure they are coated in the marinade. Lay them on the hot grill and grill for around 5–6 minutes on each side, until well charred, basting with the remaining marinade a couple of times.

Serve immediately, with lemon wedges to squeeze over.

Salt-Baked Sea Bream
with Parsley Salad

SERVES 4

2 large sea bream (approx. 500–600g
    each), scaled and gutted
2 bay leaves
a couple of handfuls of fresh herbs –
    parsley, fennel fronds or dill
2–3kg cheap table salt

The parsley salad
1 tablespoon white wine vinegar
2 banana shallots, peeled, halved and
    sliced into paper-fine half-moons
120g bunch of fresh flat-leaf parsley
2 tablespoons capers, drained
    of brine, chopped
2 tablespoons raisins, plumped
    in warm water
1 teaspoon sherry vinegar
2 tablespoons olive oil
sea salt and black pepper

Carry the tray of salt-baked fish to the table, crack the crust and peel off the shards of hard salt. Inside the fish will be sweet, moist and perfect.

I chose to use sea bream for this recipe but sea bass and turbot are also good cooked in this way. I usually keep the fins, head and tail on whole fish, and it's especially good to keep them for this dish, so the skin acts as a barrier to direct contact with the salt. This dish goes very well with the lemon and potatoes on page 88.

Heat the oven to 200°C/180°C fan/gas 6.

Rinse the fish and pat dry. Stuff the cavity of each fish with a bay leaf and a good handful of herbs. Find an ovenproof dish large enough to take the fish with a little room to spare. Line the dish with foil and cover the base with salt to around 1cm deep. Place the fish on the salt and continue to mound up the salt around and on top of the fish until they are completely buried. The amount of salt you need depends on the size of the dish. Place the dish in the oven and cook for 25–30 minutes. To test if the fish is ready, insert a skewer into the centre, count slowly to 5, then remove it and carefully test the warmth of the skewer against your lips. If it's hot, the fish is done.

While the fish is cooking, make the parsley salad. First sprinkle ½ teaspoon of the white wine vinegar over the sliced shallots in a small bowl. Then prepare the parsley. Wash it well and dry it thoroughly, then strip the leaves from the stalks. If the parsley is soft and the leaves small there is no need to chop further, but if the leaves are larger it's best to chop it a little. Toss the parsley with the capers and raisins, muddle through the rest of the white wine vinegar and the sherry vinegar, together with the olive oil, then season with salt and pepper. Squeeze any surplus vinegar out of the shallots and add them to the salad.

When the fish is ready, take a knife and crack the salt crust gently along the centre of the fish. Slip in the knife blade and peel it away from the surface. It may be easier to peel the skin away at this juncture because the idea is not to let the mass of salt taint the sweetness of the fish. Once you have exposed the fish, you can divide it into fillets in the normal way.

Lemon & Potatoes

SERVES 4

400–500g new potatoes,
   scrubbed but not peeled
1 unwaxed lemon
50g butter
sea salt and black pepper

MARCH TO JULY FOR
BEST NEW POTATOES

Credit for this recipe must go to my dear friends Tiffany and Laurent Giudicelli, who fed Jamie and me this dish years ago, one of the many, many memorable dishes that came from their generous kitchen. The tang of lemon and the gooey caramelized rinds combine beautifully with the soft potato. It is very good with grilled fish or the salt-baked sea bream on page 86. The potatoes and lemons should be sliced to a consistent thickness. A mandolin makes the job easy.

Scrub the potatoes and slice them very finely, as you would for a dauphinoise – around 2-3mm thick.

Halve the lemon lengthways and remove the knobbly top and bottom. Slice the lemon into 2-3mm half-moon slices.

Heat the oven to 200°C/180°C fan/gas 6.

Take a shallow ovenproof dish (mine was a 32cm oval) and, using a little of the butter, grease the base and sides. Assemble the dish by arranging a row of potato slices across the end of the dish, propped up at a steep angle (around 45 degrees). Against this row, prop a couple of slices of lemon, rind side up. Tuck in a couple of slivers of butter and a light seasoning of salt and pepper. Continue to assemble in this way, row by row, until the dish is full. It will have a pretty scalloped look to it.

Dot a few more tiny knobs of butter over the top and add more seasoning if you like. Place some foil over, seal well around the edges, and pop into the hot oven for around 30 minutes, until the potatoes are tender to the tip of a knife. Then remove the foil and continue to cook for 30–40 more minutes, until the potatoes and lemons are browned and caramelized. Baste with the pooled butter during the cooking time to help browning.

Mackerel Escabeche
with Wild Fennel

SERVES 8

2 or 3 big stems of wild fennel
    with fronds (around 60g)
8 tablespoons olive oil
2 red onions, peeled and sliced
    into half-moons
4 cloves of garlic, peeled and
    finely sliced
4 fresh bay leaves
½–1 teaspoon chilli flakes,
    depending on their strength
a pinch of saffron, crumbled
200ml dry white wine
4 tablespoons white wine vinegar
100ml water
80g currants
sea salt and black pepper
4 very fresh medium to large
    mackerel, cleaned, filleted
    and pin-boned
4 tablespoons semolina
3 tablespoons sunflower seeds,
    toasted until golden in a dry pan
8 slices of sourdough toast for serving

APRIL TO DECEMBER FOR MACKEREL

This dish reminds me a little of unreconstructed sardines on toast from the '50s and '60s – rarely seen now – while generously betraying its multicultural origins and sophistication. Take some thick, buttered slices of crunchy sourdough toast, arrange a portion of the fish with its accompaniments on top, and finish with a few fennel fronds and some toasted sunflower seeds. It is an ideal pick-me-up after richer indulgences.

Wild fennel (not to be confused with Florence fennel, a fattened stem often called a bulb) grows in the garden and on roadsides. It sometimes appears in the herb section of shops and definitely in garden centres, but if you can't find it, add 1 teaspoon of coarsely ground fennel seeds along with the bay leaves and finish the dish with a handful of roughly chopped dill.

Prepare ahead.

Finely slice the fat stems of the wild fennel and reserve the fronds. Heat half the olive oil in a frying pan and soften and colour the sliced fennel, onions and garlic over a medium heat for around 10–15 minutes. Add the bay leaves, chilli and saffron and stir for another minute or so. Pour in the wine, vinegar and water and bring to the boil. Add the currants, then reduce the heat and simmer gently for 7–8 minutes. Season with salt and pepper and set aside.

Season the mackerel fillets well with salt and pepper and dredge them in the semolina. Heat a couple of tablespoons of olive oil in a clean frying pan over a very high heat until shimmering.

Colour 4 of the fillets for a couple of minutes on each side in the pan. Don't worry if they're not quite cooked through. Transfer them to a wide serving dish and repeat with the remaining fish.

Pour the onion mixture and all its liquid over the fried fish. Let sit for an hour, or, even better, chill overnight and then bring back to room temperature, ready to serve on toast, sprinkled with the toasted sunflower seeds and saved fennel fronds.

Clam & Seaweed Chowder

SERVES 4 AS A SMALL BOWL,
2 HUNGRY PEOPLE

4–5 10cm pieces of dried kombu

1 handful of whole dried dulse
(or 1 rounded tablespoon
dulse flakes)

2kg clams

125ml sake (or a medium dry
white wine)

2 leeks, trimmed, halved lengthways
and washed well

150g piece of smoked pancetta, rind
removed, cut into thin lardons

25g butter

1 fat clove of garlic, peeled
and very finely chopped

1 fresh bay leaf

1 good sprig of fresh thyme

300g new potatoes, scrubbed but
not peeled, cut into 2cm cubes

150ml double cream

freshly ground black pepper

SEPTEMBER TO MAY FOR CLAMS

This soup uses two seaweeds, combined with little, sweet clams in a creamy, rich and intensely savoury bowl, with tastes of smoke and ocean.

Kombu, or edible kelp, is widely used in Japanese cooking as a key ingredient of dashi, the backbone of many Japanese broths and simmered dishes. As such, kombu is now available in many places. The second seaweed is the less well-known dulse (*Palmaria palmata*), a purple North Atlantic seaweed that tastes remarkably of bacon and has a deep, smoky umami quality.

If you can find them, use whole pieces of dried dulse. Take one handful and soak it for 5 minutes in lukewarm water from the tap, then drain and chop into small pieces. Dulse flakes may be substituted and need no additional preparation. It's important to find good, small and sweet clams. Palourde (the vongole clam) is a lovely one to choose. Do try to find sake – white wine can substitute, but won't blend so well with the seaweeds.

Soak the dried kombu in hot water from the kettle for a few seconds to soften, then drain and slice crossways into very fine strips. Put these into a saucepan with 2 litres of water, bring to the boil, then simmer gently for around an hour. Then prepare the dulse as above.

Wash the clams in cold water and drain, discarding any that refuse to shut when sharply tapped or that have damaged shells. Heat a large saucepan, throw in the clams immediately followed by the sake, clamp on the lid and cook over a high heat for about 4 minutes, shaking the pan occasionally, until the clams have popped open. Strain the juice off the clams into a bowl using a colander or sieve lined with damp muslin. Pick the meat out of about half to two-thirds of the clams and discard the shells – the remaining clams will be added to the soup in their shells.

Cut off 4–5cm from the pale green sections of the leeks and slice very finely. Cut the rest of the leeks in half lengthways, then slice into quarter-moons. Brown the pancetta lardons in butter in a medium pan until starting to crisp. Add the white pieces of sliced leek to the pan and continue until they are totally soft, around 15 minutes. Add the garlic with the bay and thyme, and soften well for a couple more minutes.

Add enough of the kombu broth (with the sliced kombu in it) to the clam juices to make up to 1 litre. Add this to the pot with the diced potatoes and the dulse. Simmer very gently for 20–30 minutes, uncovered. The intention is to cook the potatoes longer than normal and slowly, softening and loosening the starch to thicken the soup. Remove the bay and thyme.

Pour in the cream and gently simmer for a couple of minutes, then add the reserved clam meat and the clams in their shells and bring back to a simmer. Taste to check the seasoning. It probably won't need salt but will benefit from several grinds of black pepper. Serve immediately, with a scattering of very finely sliced pale green leek on top.

GATHER COOK FEAST

Gin Cured Mackerel

SERVES 6 TO START
A MEAL OR AS A SNACK

2 teaspoons black peppercorns

1 heaped teaspoon juniper berries

1 teaspoon coriander seeds

150g pure fine sea salt (fine and
    sea are important here)

100g white granulated sugar

1 unwaxed lemon

2 tablespoons gin

4 really fresh mackerel fillets,
    pin-boned (around 350g)

APRIL TO DECEMBER
FOR MACKEREL

Simple, 2–3-day-cured mackerel – fresh-from-the-boat fish, filleted, pin-boned and submerged in a botanical mix of lemon, juniper and coriander with gin. It's so easy: I make it all the time.

Slice the finished mackerel thinly for eating on rye bread with crème fraîche, lemon, dill and cucumber, or with the pressed parsley potatoes on page 39. Good with a large gin and tonic in hand.

Coarsely grind the peppercorns, juniper and coriander in a mortar and pestle. Mix the spices with the salt and sugar in a medium bowl. Zest over about half the lemon. Add the gin and stir around to make a damp, sandy sludge.

Choose a small plastic food box that will hold the mackerel in two snug layers (if you are worried about pervasive fishy smells, line it with clingfilm). Cover the base with some of the cure mix, then lay in 2 fillets, skin down. Cover these with more of the cure, laying the last 2 fillets on top, skin up. Cover the top with the remaining cure mix so that all the fish is in contact with it.

Cover and refrigerate for 2–3 days. The shorter curing time will result in a slightly fresher, softer texture. The longer cure will impart more flavour to the fish and its flesh will become increasingly firm and translucent.

Remove the fillets from the salty sludge. Briefly rinse under cold running water, then pat dry with kitchen paper. If cured for the full 3 days, the fillets will keep, wrapped in clingfilm, for a week in the fridge.

Salt Marsh Lamb Chops with Sherried Capers & Sea Greens

SERVES 4

4 large salt marsh lamb chops
   (around 550g)
sea salt and black pepper
some chopped fresh thyme leaves
2 tablespoons olive oil
300g beet tops, chard or foraged
   sea beet, washed and chopped
50g samphire, washed
   (if not using sea beet)
40g butter
2 good tablespoons capers,
   drained of brine, chopped
2 anchovy fillets, chopped
150ml Oloroso or similar rich sherry

To serve
a good quantity of buttery
   mashed potatoes

JUNE TO SEPTEMBER FOR
SALT MARSH LAMB

The marshes of the Lleyn and Gower peninsulas near where I live are used to graze flocks of sheep in the early spring to summer months. Meat grazed on this sea-sprayed and herb-rich pasture is sweeter than normal, with a slight salt-savoury tang.

The perfect accompaniment to this lamb is sea beet, which is common around the shingly coasts of England and Wales and easy to identify, with a deep and more intense flavour similar to all its garden descendants. If you are far from the coast, fake it by using sea beet's closest cultivated descendants, beetroot tops or chard, together with samphire for an extra iodine kick.

If you live near the coast where alexanders grow, you could also pair these chops with this delicious foraged ingredient. (Instructions for preparing alexanders follow on page 98.)

This is a quick and excellent supper or lunch dish and is really good eaten with a deep pile of pillowy, buttery mashed potatoes.

Allow the chops to come to room temperature by seasoning them with sea salt, black pepper and some chopped fresh thyme and leaving them in a dish for an hour to absorb the flavours.

Make the mash the way you like it and keep it warm.

Pour the olive oil into a good heavy frying pan – it should cover the base of the pan with a thin layer. Heat the pan over a medium heat until the oil is starting to shiver a little. Lay the chops in the pan and brown for 2–3 minutes on each side, then turn on to the fatty edge and brown for 2–3 minutes. Test the chops with your finger at this point – they should be quite soft still, which means they will still be very pink inside. Put a lid on the pan and continue to cook for a couple more minutes on each side, until golden. Test with your finger again, a slight firmness indicates they are cooked a little more but still pink. Remove the chops to rest, covered.

The beet leaves and samphire (if using) should still be damp from washing, so they can steam in their own moisture. Throw them into a dry, hot pan, clap the lid on and steam, turning occasionally, until tender. Finish with a knob of butter.

GATHER COOK FEAST

While the beets are cooking, pour away the oil from the chop pan and melt 30g of the butter over a medium heat, adding the capers and anchovies and turning to soften a little. Then pour in the sherry – the pan will spit and sizzle. Reduce the sherry to half.

Spoon the mashed potatoes, then the greens and finally the chops on to warm plates.

Add the juices that will have seeped from the chops to the sherry mix and add a dash more sherry if needed. Give the whole a second or two more bubbling over the heat, then dribble it equally over all the plated chops.

Preparing Alexanders

The pale green-flowered alexanders plant is common on the coasts of Cornwall, Pembrokeshire and Dorset, growing along the foot of wall banks and on pathways and roads. The plant has a pungent, almost fetid smell, but the boiled and buttered leaves and stems have a delicately perfumed myrrh-like fragrance. They are delicious. It is important to identify the plant accurately, using a trusted guidebook or teacher, because there are quite a few toxic umbellifers to avoid. Fortunately alexanders are one of the easiest in the umbellifer family to learn about and identify.
You can eat all the soft leaves and the soft parts of the stem. Peel the skin off the stems in ribbons (somewhat like peeling rhubarb), slice the stems into logs, boil for a few minutes until tender, then toss with some butter, salt and pepper. Serve alongside roast lamb or fish; or make a risotto with blue cheese and alexanders; or combine with apple and spicy walnuts in a salad.

Pickled Samphire

MAKES 1 X 500ML JAR

320ml white wine vinegar

50g white granulated sugar

40g soft brown sugar

1 heaped teaspoon yellow
   mustard seeds

heaped ½ teaspoon celery seeds

heaped ¼ teaspoon turmeric

2 cloves

280g young tender samphire,
   washed and drained well

JUNE TO AUGUST
FOR MARSH SAMPHIRE

Pickling marsh samphire is easy; the only proviso is to find young and tender samphire early in the season. Taking time to pickle only to have a mouthful of stringiness is frustrating. To check, chew a few bits raw or drop a strand or two into boiling water and nibble when tender.

Eat this deliciousness alongside the potted rabbit (see page 194) on toasted spelt sourdough (see page 199).

Choose a smallish saucepan that will be big enough to hold all the samphire. Combine the vinegar, sugars and spices in the pan. You won't need to add any additional salt, as the samphire itself is plenty salty. Bring the pickling liquid to a boil and simmer for a couple of minutes to dissolve the sugar. Add the samphire, bring back to a boil and simmer for another 2 minutes.

Use a slotted spoon to pack the samphire into a hot, sterile jar (see page 105 for instructions) and pour over the hot pickling liquid until submerged. Seal immediately.

Store somewhere cool and dark and use within a year. Wait at least a couple of weeks before eating any, as the spice flavours need some time to develop. Once opened, keep in the fridge and eat within a couple of weeks.

Pickled Herring

SERVES 4–6 AS A
STARTER OR SNACK

200–300g fine sea salt

6 very fresh fillets of herring
(around 300g), scaled and
partially pin-boned

175ml white wine vinegar

175ml water

175g white sugar

2 dried bay leaves

1 teaspoon black peppercorns

1 teaspoon yellow mustard seeds

½ teaspoon allspice berries

¼ teaspoon cloves

1 small red onion, peeled and sliced

1 small carrot, peeled and sliced

3 good sprigs of fresh dill

APRIL TO DECEMBER
FOR HERRING

Following ancient northern European tradition, herring are first cured in salt then pickled in a sweet-sour pickling liquid. They are delicious on thinly sliced sourdough wheat or rye bread spread with butter or mustard and topped with pickled vegetables and dill; or with boiled potatoes, cornichons and crème fraîche; or with split, warm soft-boiled eggs.

Herring are cheap, can be very sustainable (but check latest information) and are under-appreciated. So low is the demand for them that they can be hard to find. Ask your fishmonger to look out for them. Herring are impossible to pin-bone entirely. Have a go yourself or ask your fishmonger to remove the biggest bones, but don't expect perfection. You won't notice the small bones once pickled. Make sure the fillets have been trimmed of their fins, tails and ribcages.

You will need a suitable 500ml sterile glass jar (see page 105). If you care (as I do) about how the herring look in the jar, slice the carrots and onion for maximum effect. A jar of pickled herring makes a more interesting and useful gift than ubiquitous chutney, so make it look lovely too.

Take a plastic food box just big enough to hold 3 of the fillets lying side by side and line with clingfilm. Cover the base with a third of the salt. Lay 3 fillets, skin side down, in the bottom. Spoon over another third of the salt to cover, lay over the other 3 fillets, skin side up, and cover with the remaining salt so that all the flesh is in contact with plenty of salt. Cover and place in the coldest part of the fridge for at least 1 week and up to 6. The longer you leave the herring the paler the flesh goes and the sweeter the fish smells and tastes.

Place the vinegar, water, sugar, bay leaves and spices in a small non-reactive saucepan and bring to the boil, stirring to dissolve the sugar. Remove from the heat and leave to steep and cool.

Lift the fish out of its salty sludge and place it in a bowl of cold water. Leave to soak for 30 minutes to an hour, longer if you left the herring in the salt for the full 6 weeks.

Remove the herring from the water and pat dry with kitchen paper. If you like, remove the skin at this point, or leave them with the skin on

GATHER COOK FEAST

as they do in Scandinavia. There is no need for the fillets to be perfectly skinned, as you will hardly notice it at the end. You can leave the herring whole or cut them into sections.

When the jar and pickling liquid have both cooled completely, assemble the pickled herring. Layer the pieces of herring, skin side down if you have left the skins on, in the sterilized jar along with the sliced onion and carrot and the sprigs of dill. Pack them in neatly without breaking them. Pour over the pickling liquid, including the spices, to cover the fish completely, and close the jar. You may not need quite all the liquid. Store in the fridge for a week before using and use within a month.

Sterilizing Jars & Bottles

Many of the recipes in this book require a sterile jar or bottle. Here are a couple of easy ways to achieve this.

A useful, simple method for short-term storage or for recipes using vinegars or alcohol is to put the clean jars, lids or bottles into a dishwasher and run it on a very hot cycle. Leave them in until you are ready to use them. Time the cycle so that it finishes just when the jars are dry, but still hot, to avoid them cracking when you fill them with hot produce.

A preferred method for complete sterilization is to put clean jars into a cold oven and turn it to 160°C/140°C fan/gas 3. Once the oven has reached temperature, leave them inside for at least 15 minutes. Use the jars straight from the hot oven when filling with a hot preserve to prevent them cracking, or leave them to cool undisturbed if they are to be filled cold. Boil any lids or rubber sealing rings in water for 10 minutes. This method makes it easier to match the temperature of the jar to your produce – making for a sterile seal and avoiding glass fractures.

Sea Buckthorn
Burnt Cream

MAKES 4 SMALL (100ML) RAMEKINS

4 egg yolks
40g caster sugar
a pinch of sea salt
300ml double cream
4 tablespoons sea buckthorn juice
4 teaspoons caster sugar
   for the crackly top

Reaching far out into the sea between the Loughor and the Towy estuaries in Wales is a wide long beach – undulating white dunes fringed with pines – which is also host to impenetrable, prickly ranks of blue-grey-leaved sea buckthorn. I don't know if the planting was intentional, to stabilize the dunes, as with marram grass, or if it colonized of its own accord, but in September dense clusters of the bright orange berries form and go largely ignored, fading and whitening as the year progresses.

Sea buckthorn berries are super-sour, with a payload of vitamin C and beta-carotene that outstrips the humble orange and carrot. They squash in the hand when collecting, so squeeze the juice directly from the bush into a container, rather than attempt to pick like blackberries. If you'd rather, buy the juice from a specialist supplier (see page 336).

Temper the sourness with an onslaught of full dairy richness, either in a cheesecake with white chocolate, or here in a classic burnt cream made with a high proportion of eggs and double cream.

Heat the oven to 180°C/160°C fan/gas 4.

In a medium bowl, briefly whisk the egg yolks with the caster sugar and a pinch of salt. Bring the cream to the boil, remove from the heat immediately and pour the scalding cream over the sugar and egg mixture, whisking as you pour. Add the sea buckthorn juice and mix well.

Pour the mixture into four small ramekins and put them into a roasting tin big enough for all four. Carefully pour enough cold water into the tin to reach three-quarters of the way up the ramekins. Bake in the oven for 35–40 minutes, until they are slightly set but still wobbly to the touch (they will continue to cook in residual heat once out of the oven). Leave them to cool, then refrigerate for an hour or so or leave overnight.

Before you bring them to the table, scatter a teaspoon of caster sugar on each and blast with a blowtorch (or under a grill, but a blowtorch is better) until the sugar is caramelized, bubbling and crunchy. If using a grill, leave to cool in the fridge for an hour before serving: one of the joys of burnt cream is the contrast of cool custard with crunch, and such pleasure is lost if the ramekin is still warm from the grill.

GATHER COOK FEAST

Two Salted
Ice Creams

EACH RECIPE SERVES 4

For the salted chocolate ice cream
200g full cream milk
200g double cream
2 level teaspoons Maldon sea salt
130g golden caster sugar
150g 70% dark chocolate,
    finely chopped

For the salted peanut ice cream
200g full cream milk
130g golden caster sugar
150g salted crunchy peanut butter
200g double cream
50g dark chocolate, finely chopped
50g well-salted peanuts,
    roughly chopped

Ice cream is for the seaside and salt is for the sea, thus two simple, salted ice creams for imagining you are tucked away in the dunes. These two go well served together – salty peanut with chocolate is like an ice cream Snickers bar.

Salted Chocolate Ice Cream

Warm the milk, cream, salt and caster sugar in a pan, heating until nearly simmering and stirring until the sugar is fully dissolved. Scatter over the finely chopped chocolate. Let it sit for one minute and stir to partly dissolve the chocolate. Set aside to cool.

Churn in an ice cream maker until thick, following the manufacturer's instructions. Scoop out into a plastic snap-top container and freeze. This is a soft ice cream, which will scoop directly from the freezer.

Salted Peanut Ice Cream

Warm the milk and caster sugar in a pan, stirring until the sugar is fully dissolved. Add the warm milk gradually to the peanut butter, stirring to make a creamy paste.

Allow the mixture to cool to lukewarm, then stir in the cream, chopped chocolate and chopped peanuts.

Churn in an ice cream maker until thick, following the manufacturer's instructions. Scoop out into a plastic snap-top container and freeze.

Buttermilk Ice Cream

130g caster sugar
a pinch of sea salt
200ml buttermilk
200ml double cream

The simplest of ice creams, fresh and bright, with a tangy, dairy flavour, making it a pure and satisfying partner for soft, sweet and sticky desserts. Try it with the plum and walnut tart on page 265, or the rough apple pie on page 324. For a quick pairing, wrap sweet plums in foil with soft brown sugar, cinnamon and star anise and bake.

Buttermilk is a relatively ignored ingredient and traditionally made buttermilk is hard to find. It's made naturally as a by-product of traditional slow butter production, a gentle fermentation happening over some days. Modern versions use a similar culture added artificially.

Combine the sugar and salt with the buttermilk in a pan and place over a medium heat to dissolve the sugar, stirring well to combine. Don't let the mixture boil. Remove from the heat, allow the mixture to cool a little, then add the double cream, stirring well to remove any clumps of cream that lurk in the mix.

Churn in an ice cream maker according to the manufacturer's instructions until set. Scoop out into a plastic container and freeze. Or follow the instructions below for making by hand.

Ice Cream without an Ice Cream Maker

If you don't have an ice cream maker you can still make ice cream by hand. Put the cool finished mixture into the freezer in a plastic box. Every 2–3 hours, give it a good stir and put it back, continuing until it is softly set. At this point take it out again and beat it well with an electric whisk, returning it to the freezer until completely frozen. All ice creams are best eaten within 3 weeks of being put into the freezer.

Saffron Buns

MAKES 12 BUNS

500g strong white flour

10g sea salt

20g dried yeast (not fast-acting)

70g raisins

50g candied peel, chopped
  into small pieces

finely grated zest of 1 orange

150ml water

150ml milk

60g caster sugar

100g butter, in small cubes

1 lightly packed teaspoon
  saffron strands

1 egg, beaten with a pinch of sea salt

sprinkle of caster sugar for glazing

Saffron cakes are common across the Mediterranean and in Scandinavia, but in the British Isles they survive mostly in Cornwall. For me the taste is associated with fresh, salty Easter holidays next to the churning sea and rocky coves of that English county.

This recipe combines the qualities of a hot cross bun with Cornish saffron cake, to make an alternative Easter morning bake. Break them open when still warm from the oven to savour the deep fragrance of the yellow saffron with the tang of orange zest and candied peel.

Put the flour into a large mixing bowl and leave in a warm place to reach room temperature. Then add the salt, yeast, dried fruit and zest of orange.

Warm the water, milk, sugar and butter in a small saucepan until all combined and the sugar has melted. Take off the heat and add the saffron strands to the liquid, leaving to steep in a warm place until it's reached blood temperature.

Make a well in the centre of the flour and pour in the blood-heat liquid. Mix together with a rubber spatula, scraping around the sides until the liquid is fully incorporated and you have a thick doughy paste.

Drop the dough on to a board and knead well, slapping it down, stretching a length towards you with a hand either side and folding back the pleat to trap air. Keep going like this for at least 10 minutes. This dough and your hands will be very sticky but as you knead it will get easier to manage. Use your rubber spatula to scrape the board and yourself. You will know when you have kneaded enough because the dough will become flexible and springy. Test by pressing with a floury finger – if the dough is ready the finger mark will spring back. Form the dough into a large bun shape by pinching all the edges together and then turning it smooth side up.

Give the mixing bowl a wipe, oil it a little, then settle the dough inside, cover with a tea towel and move the bowl to a warm, draught-free place to rise. The aim is for the dough to double in size. How long that takes depends on the ambient temperature. In a moderately warm room, allow 1–2 hours, or longer in a cooler place.

Once the dough has doubled in size, tip it out of the bowl and cut it into twelve equal-sized lumps. Make into little bun shapes by tucking the edges under the bun base and pinching to seal. Arrange the buns, smooth side up and spaced well apart, on baking trays covered with baking paper. Return to the warm place to prove for a second time for 30 minutes to 1 hour, until the buns look pillowy and have risen to 1½ times their original size.

Heat the oven to 220°C/200°C fan/gas 7.

When the buns have risen nicely, use the beaten egg to glaze the tops and sprinkle with a little caster sugar. Bake in the oven for 12–15 minutes, until golden. To be sure the buns are completely cooked, tap on the base. A cooked bun will sound hollow.

Eat warm on the day of baking, spread with good butter.

Lemon Thyme Granita

SERVES 6

250ml water
200g white granulated sugar
a pinch of sea salt
10g fresh lemon thyme sprigs
   (a good handful)
165ml lemon juice (probably 3 lemons)
grated lemon zest (optional), to serve

There is something reminiscent of juice-filled, dripping-on-the-hand lollipops about this granita – eaten on the way home from school on a hot day (why did those days always happen before the summer holidays began?). Plant some lemon thyme, which you can find most easily in garden centres, its pretty variegated leaves used as a decorative border.

Choose a hot day to serve this.

In a small saucepan heat the water, sugar and salt gently until the sugar has dissolved. Add the lemon thyme, then remove from the heat and set aside to steep for at least half an hour, until the syrup has cooled and tastes strongly of thyme.

Add the lemon juice, then strain the mixture into a shallow dish (metal is good) and cover. Freeze until crystals start to form around the edge. Check after an hour, use a fork to stir the mixture and disperse the crystals, then return to the freezer. Fork the granita every hour or so until it becomes the texture of snow, about another 4–6 hours depending on the dish and your freezer.

This sweet granita will not set hard, so you'll be able to scoop it straight from the freezer. Perhaps finish with some grated zest of lemon on the top.

HOE WATER SOFT

EGGS **HOME GROUND**

CHICKEN BEAN

RASPBERRY TENDER

RIPE PEAS SOW

HERBS GERMINATE

LAVENDER CREAMY

ELDERFLOWER

BEES FRAGRANT

BLOSSOM SUGAR

The word 'garden' comes from the Saxon word geard, meaning fenced or enclosed: a protected space where we may cultivate on a domestic scale. This could be anything from a tiny window box or modest allotment to a magnificent walled garden of several acres. The scale doesn't matter. More important is our deep-seated impulse to cultivate: to sow a seed, water, protect and then harvest when the time is right. A garden can be made anywhere and any size, not only in the countryside but also in the city, where just a scrap of space could accommodate a tub of soil to grow some peas, a few carrots or a lettuce.

The middle of summer is when the riot of vegetables sown in the surge of spring finally starts to come to fruition. Take a colander to your plot and see what can be turned into supper. I cook in a much less structured way at this time of year, seeing what's available, working to the crop. The colander gets filled and is taken into the kitchen to turn into supper. It could be a bowl of peas and Feta; or a grating of courgette, which turns into a fritter. Quite often it is a salad of one sort or another. Supper preparation often merges into an unplanned hour or so in the garden.

This chapter is largely a celebration of the vegetable, with a little nod to chicken. It starts with a trio of wonderfully intense soups and a scatter of salads. There are fragrant custard pies made using gooseberries, fennel or camomile, and an updated bread and butter pudding with bursts of raspberry set in creamy brioche. Shredded nasturtiums are whipped into butter for potatoes, roses into macaroons, lavender into a cake, elderflower cordial made in a way that preserves all its drowsy woodsy-ness.

Eat lightly and easily – enjoy the summer.

Chilled Beetroot Soup

SERVES 6

1kg beetroot
extra virgin olive oil
sea salt and black pepper
500g ripe and flavoursome
    tomatoes, cored and
    roughly chopped
1 ripe red bell pepper, stemmed,
    deseeded and roughly chopped
1 medium red onion, peeled
    and roughly chopped
1 baby cucumber, peeled
    and roughly chopped
2 fairly fat cloves of garlic,
    peeled and crushed to a paste
1 big slice of good bread
    (stale is fine), crusts removed,
    torn into pieces
1 tablespoon red wine vinegar
1–2 tablespoons aged sherry
    vinegar

To finish
walnut oil or extra virgin olive oil
a few broken, toasted walnuts
fresh white goat's cheese

This recipe is inspired by the traditional Spanish gazpacho, but is given new and vibrant life using beetroot. The trick is to roast half the beetroot to bring out its lush sweetness and to grate the rest raw to keep its vibrant colour and fresh taste. Combined with the ripe tomatoes, pepper and onion, it has a flavour sweet, sour and earthy all at once. If you can leave it a day before eating, the flavours will be even better developed.

Heat the oven to 220°C/200°C fan/gas 7.

Place half the beetroot in a single layer in a small roasting tin, dribble over a little oil, sprinkle with salt and pour in a finger's depth of water. Cover very tightly with foil, crimping it around the edges to stop the steam escaping. Bake in the oven until a paring knife will easily slip into the centre of the biggest beet. This will take about an hour (more if they are large).

While the beetroot are roasting, prepare all the other vegetables. Peel and grate the remaining 500g of beetroot. Mix the grated beetroot in a big bowl together with all the other ingredients bar the two vinegars. Add a generous sprinkling of salt and a good slug of olive oil.

While the roasted beetroot are still warm, rub off their skins, chop them up, sprinkle with the red wine vinegar, then mix them into the bowl with everything else. If you can, leave the bowl to sit in the fridge for an hour or so or overnight: the flavours will combine and integrate wonderfully.

Blitz the mixture in batches, using a jug blender or immersion blender, to a really smooth purée, adding another good glug of olive oil and some cold water to thin it a little if needed (it should be just thin enough to run off a spoon). Taste and season with salt, pepper and sherry vinegar as needed.

Chill thoroughly before serving. Check the seasoning once more and serve with a little dribbled walnut oil, some toasted walnuts and a crumble of white goat's cheese.

Chilled Cucumber & Dill Soup
with Crushed Walnuts

SERVES 4

80g walnut halves

450g good natural yoghurt

2 cloves of garlic, peeled and
      crushed smooth

1 tablespoon extra virgin olive oil

1 tablespoon walnut oil,
      plus a little more to finish

a small bunch of fresh dill
      (around 20g), finely chopped,
      plus a little more to finish

around 200ml cold water

sea salt

250g mini cucumbers

1 tablespoon lemon juice

MIDDLE TO LATE SUMMER
FOR MINI CUCUMBERS

We have forgotten the taste of a good cucumber, habituated as we are to the hydroponically grown, ramrod-straight, selected-for-shelf-life versions in our weekly shop. A few years ago I had reason to visit a remote area of Georgia called Tusheti National Park, where the only access road was a single-lane dirt track which wound precipitously through the mountains for 10 hours before dropping to the valley floor. The sequestered nature of this land fosters a flora and fauna so rich, so diverse, you might think yourself in Eden. There I ate cucumbers grown in the black, rich soil of the garden belonging to the ramshackle house where we stayed. They were intensely cucumber-y, tasting like a memory of a cucumber I have never had. The closest you could get to this wonderment is to track down the thin-skinned mini cucumbers that have less water, more taste and ripen in the middle to late summer.

Yoghurt, cucumber, garlic and walnuts are a wonderful combination in a cool bowl for a hot day. If it is very hot, you can even add a couple of ice cubes to the bowl.

Preheat the oven to 200°C/180°C fan/gas 6 and toast the walnuts on a tray for around 8 minutes, until golden and rubbable. Tip on to a clean tea towel, gather up into a bag and rub vigorously to loosen the skins. Pick out the pieces of nut, leaving the skins behind. Chop very finely.

Beat together the yoghurt, crushed garlic and oils until smooth and well combined. Stir in the nuts and dill (keeping back a little of each to finish the bowls). Stir in the cold water until the soup is a lovely consistency – something between thin and thick cream is nice – then season to taste with salt. Chill the soup in the fridge for at least an hour.

Cut the cucumbers into very fine dice (as tiny as you can make them) and layer in a colander with light sprinklings of salt. Leave for 20–30 minutes, so that the salt draws out the excess water from the cucumbers. The salt will also season them and help keep colour and texture.

Just before serving, stir the cucumber and lemon juice into the yoghurt mixture and check the seasoning once more. Finish the bowls of soup with the few walnuts and dill you have kept aside and dribble over a few drops of walnut oil.

Lettuce & Lovage Soup

SERVES 4 AS A STARTER
OR 2 HUNGRY BEASTS

400g good-quality lettuce, washed
    and spun dry, keeping outer leaves
a handful of lovage leaves –
    around 10–15g
2 large banana shallots, peeled
    and very finely sliced
25g butter
600ml good chicken stock
a good handful of garden peas –
    frozen are fine
2–3 tablespoons single cream
1 tablespoon lemon juice,
    plus a little more for serving
sea salt and black pepper

For this soup it is very important to search out a good, earthy, structured lettuce with dark green outer leaves. Organic is preferable. The slightly bitter outer leaves enable this soup to hold its own – pale supermarket offerings will not have the same impact. If you can, find large floppy, dark green oak-leaf or butterhead lettuce or try a big, dark Cos or Little Gem. See page 33 for information about lovage.

It is important to liquidize this one – the process seems to extract maximum taste and juices as well as enabling a silky, smooth texture.

To prepare the lettuce, strip off all the leaves from the core stem and check for damage and creepy-crawlies. Rinse well in cool water and spin dry. There is no need to waste any leaves, but judiciously trim off any brown bits and chop the central core into small chunks so everything cooks at a similar rate. Then bundle all the leaves together and finely slice across into strips.

To prepare the lovage, strip the leaves off any remaining stems, rinse, spin dry, then finely shred. You can keep the stems for a stock later on. Keep aside a small pile of even more finely shredded lovage for serving.

In a medium sturdy pan, soften the shallots in the melted butter over a gentle heat, stirring often until transparent – around 5 minutes.

Add the shredded lettuce and lovage and continue to soften until the leaves look limp and start to give off some of their juices.

Add the stock and the peas and continue to cook on a slow bubble for 5–10 minutes more.

Take off the heat and cool a little, then liquidize to a fine texture. Return to the pan and add the cream and lemon juice. Season to taste with salt and pepper.

Warm through very gently. Then serve in small bowls, topped with a little bunch of very finely shredded lovage.

New Season Carrot & Beetroot Salad with Orange & Cumin

SERVES 4

500g young beetroot
    and their leaves, washed well
olive oil
flaky sea salt
500g young carrots,
    peeled (or scrubbed if baby)
    and cut into shards
plain yoghurt (optional)

The dressing
zest of 1 orange, finely grated
juice of ½ an orange
2 tablespoons lemon juice
¾ teaspoon sugar
¾ teaspoon ground cumin
½ teaspoon paprika
1 small clove of garlic,
    peeled and crushed to a paste
around 50ml extra virgin olive oil
fine sea salt and black pepper

JUNE FOR NEW LITTLE
BEETROOT & CARROTS

It seems decadent to pick tiny new carrots and beetroot before they have had time to swell into more human-sustaining sizes. But the sweet flavour of adolescent roots makes the sacrifice worth it. Harvesting at various stages is one of the benefits of growing your own.

If shopping, try to find young slender bunched carrots and small firm purple beetroot with their leaves still attached (if lacking, throw in a few spinach leaves to compensate).

This goes well with just-landed, charred-in-the-pan mackerel.

Heat the oven to 220°C/200°C fan/gas 7.

Trim the tops off the beetroot and reserve, leaving just a centimetre or two of stalk. Place the beets in a single layer in a small roasting tin, trickle over a little oil, sprinkle with salt and pour in one finger's depth of water. Cover very tightly with foil and bake in the oven for about an hour, or until a paring knife slips easily into the centre. Toss the chopped carrots with a tablespoon of olive oil and a little salt and spread over a small baking tray lined with baking paper. Roast in the same oven for about 30 minutes, until tender and starting to caramelize around the edges.

Make the dressing by whisking all the ingredients together in a jug. Season to taste and add a little more oil if it seems too acidic. Divide the dressing between two bowls and when the carrots are ready, transfer them directly to one of the bowls of dressing, mix and leave until lukewarm.

When the beetroot are ready, rub their skins off and cut them into wedges while they are still warm. Transfer them directly to the second bowl of dressing and toss to combine, leaving them to marinate until lukewarm. Separate the beetroot leaves from their stalks and wash and spin dry if necessary. Blanch the leaves for just 1 minute in a pan of boiling salted water. Lift them out with a slotted spoon directly into a bowl of cold water to stop the cooking and preserve their bright colour. When cool, drain well and gently squeeze out any excess water.

Arrange the salad on a platter, building it up in layers. Repeat until everything is used up, and trickle over any remaining dressing left in the bowls if it needs more. Finish with yoghurt if you like.

Green Panzanella

2 big slices of stale white sourdough
    bread (around 150g), torn
    into small bite-sized pieces

1 small courgette (around 150g),
    peeled into fine ribbons
    with a veg peeler

1 thin-skinned mini cucumber
    (around 150g), halved lengthways
    and sliced crossways

3 spring onions, thinly sliced
    crossways (white and green parts)

4 tablespoons lemon juice,
    plus more to taste

4 tablespoons extra virgin olive oil,
    plus more to serve

½ teaspoon fine sea salt

500g broad beans
    (200g podded weight)

finely grated zest of 1 large
    unwaxed lemon

150g sugar snap peas, trimmed
    and finely sliced crossways

2 Little Gem lettuces (one if big),
    leaves torn into pieces

leaves from 6 sprigs of fresh mint

flaky sea salt and black pepper

100–150g fresh sheep's
    or goat's curd (or white soft
    goat's cheese) (optional)

My good friend Orlando described this as a 'lovely, lemony, frisky and green salad'.

Fresh, sweet garden peas could be substituted for sugar snaps. If you can't find a true fresh goat's curd, choose a log of fresh, white, soft goat's cheese from the chiller cabinet. The curd or cheese is not essential – this salad is also good without.

Mix the pieces of bread, courgette ribbons, cucumber slices, sliced spring onions, lemon juice, olive oil and ½ a teaspoon of fine sea salt in a bowl. Leave to soften for around 30–45 minutes.

Meanwhile blanch the podded broad beans in boiling salted water for a couple of minutes, until tender. Lift them out with a slotted spoon directly into a bowl of ice-cold water to stop the cooking and preserve their bright green colour. When cool, drain them and slip them out of their rubbery skins.

Once the bread has softened, add the broad beans, lemon zest, sliced sugar snap peas and torn lettuce leaves to the bowl. Stack the mint leaves in neat piles, then take each pile in turn, roll it up lengthways like a cigar and cut crossways into fine ribbons. Add the mint ribbons to the salad and toss everything together, seasoning to taste with flaky sea salt and freshly ground black pepper. Add more lemon juice to taste and a dribble or two of extra virgin olive oil for serving.

If you like, top with good blobs of fresh curd.

Courgette Fritters
with Minted Yoghurt

500g firm young courgettes,
   trimmed and grated using the
   biggest hole of a box grater
1 teaspoon fine sea salt
3 spring onions, trimmed and finely
   sliced (white and green parts)
150g Feta, crumbled
1 teaspoon dried mint
2 tablespoons very finely
   chopped fresh dill
½–1 teaspoon chilli flakes,
   depending on their heat
1 teaspoon sumac (optional)
2 eggs
50g plain flour
light olive oil or sunflower oil
sea salt and black pepper
edible garden flowers to finish
   (borage, rocket, nasturtiums
   or marigold petals) (optional)

The minted yoghurt
1 small clove of garlic, peeled
   and crushed to a paste
250g natural Greek yoghurt
sea salt
leaves from 4 good stems of
   fresh mint, sliced into ribbons
2 tablespoons extra virgin olive oil

HIGH SUMMER FOR COURGETTES

If you grow courgettes you'll know there is always a need for a new recipe to use the unceasing supply ripening on the plants. The classic recipe is here given a little twist with dill, chilli flakes and sumac and combined with minted yoghurt for a sweetly satisfying lunch or early supper. The key to success is ridding the courgettes of their excess water. All you need is crisp salad leaves alongside.

Place the grated courgettes in a colander set over a bowl and gently toss with a teaspoon of fine sea salt. Leave for half an hour to release a large quantity of bright green liquid – tip this down the sink.

For the minted yoghurt, beat the crushed garlic into the yoghurt until smooth and season with salt. Place the sliced mint in a mortar and pound with the pestle to a smooth paste. Loosen the paste with the olive oil and then swirl the green oil into the yoghurt (leaving it streaky is nice).

Squeeze the salted courgettes to rid them of water and place in a mixing bowl. Add the spring onions, cheese, herbs and spices. Crack in the eggs and mix well. Thoroughly fold in the flour.

Gloss a wide frying pan with a covering of oil and heat over a medium flame. Drop a small teaspoon of the mixture into the pan and cook on each side. Taste and adjust the seasoning in the mix as appropriate.

Carefully drop the mix into the still-hot pan to form fritters, heaped tablespoonful by heaped tablespoonful (you'll probably only fit in around 5). Cook on each side until golden brown and slightly puffed. Transfer to a plate lined with kitchen paper and keep warm while you cook the next batch.

Serve the fritters while still slightly warm, with the minted yoghurt. A few edible flowers are pretty on the side.

GATHER COOK FEAST

Broad Beans & Black
Pudding on Toast

SERVES 2

500g fresh broad beans in their
    pods (200g when podded)
sea salt and black pepper
1 small lemon, halved
1 tablespoon olive oil, plus
    some to dress
100g black pudding, skinned
    and cut into 1cm cubes
1 banana shallot, peeled and
    very finely diced
1 clove of garlic, peeled and
    very finely diced
1 teaspoon fennel seeds
2 slices of good bread –
    sourdough or brown
good-quality butter, for spreading
a few sprigs of fresh flat-leaf parsley
    or mint or lovage, finely shredded

MAY TO AUGUST FOR
FRESH BROAD BEANS

This is a simple lunch or quick supper dish of deliciousness, or a pretty starter for a communal supper. Search out excellent black pudding (very good value for the nutritional punch – see sources, page 335) and the freshest, tastiest broad beans you can find.

Even though something-on-toast sounds like the simplest dish possible, timing is everything. Swift and organized is the name of the game.

Pod the broad beans and boil them in a little salted water for 2–3 minutes. When they appear to bloat and get a little wrinkly, drain them from the water and spread them on a chopping board until cool enough to handle. To peel them, pinch one end to make a slit and squeeze the other until the bright green bean pops out. Work through the whole pile. Dress them all with a good squeeze of lemon juice and a liberal grinding of salt and pepper and leave to absorb while you get on with the rest.

Heat a dribble of the olive oil in a small frying pan and brown the cubes of black pudding, turning them with a spatula until crispy on each side, about 3–4 minutes. Remove from the pan and put on a warm plate while you cook the alliums. Add the shallot, garlic and fennel seeds to the empty pan (add a little more oil if the pan is dry) and cook until soft, tender, sweet and translucent.

While these are all cooking, toast the bread and spread with good butter. Place the toast on two warm plates.

Add a couple of cubes of black pudding and a few beans to the pan and squash them into the oniony mixture, then add the rest of the black pudding and the broad beans, gently combining them. Season the mixture with salt and pepper and another good squeeze of lemon to taste. Give it a gentle stir as it warms (don't break up the beans). Divide the mixture between the two slices of toast, scatter the shredded herbs on top and dress with olive oil and a little lemon juice if needed.

Chicken with Early Summer Vegetables

SERVES 2

400g chicken pieces, bone in
(1–2 per person depending on size)
sea salt and black pepper
300ml good chicken stock
300–350g prepared mixed early
summer vegetables – French
beans, peas, broccoli, summer
cabbage, chard, beet tops
1 tablespoon olive oil
6–7 stems of fresh thyme,
leaves stripped off
55g unsalted butter, cubed
1 banana shallot, peeled and sliced
2 cloves of garlic, peeled and sliced
6–7 stems of fresh tarragon,
leaves stripped off
1 lemon, to squeeze

JUNE TO JULY FOR TENDER
SUMMER VEGETABLES

Simply cooked tender pieces of chicken alongside succulent, new, green vegetables from the garden.

In my veggie-loving household the portion of greens is quite large and the pieces of chicken fairly modest. Feel free to adjust at will. Choose a pan that can go from oven to hob and back.

Take the chicken pieces out of the fridge, rub the skin with 1 teaspoon of salt and leave to absorb the seasoning.

Put the chicken stock into a pan and boil hard for around 12 minutes, to reduce to half its volume. Take off the heat.

Prepare all the veg thus: top and tail the French beans and cut in half across the middle; pod the fresh peas; trim the broccoli, splitting it into florets and slicing them vertically into slim shards; wash the summer cabbage leaves, remove large stalks and tear into smallish pieces; the same with the beet tops and chard, but chop the stalks small.

Heat the oven to 220°C/200°C fan/gas 7.

In your hob-to-oven lidded pot, heat the olive oil over a medium-high heat until hot, then lower the chicken pieces in, skin side down, browning until crisp and golden. Turn to do the same on all sides. This should take around 5 minutes in all. Add the thyme and 30g of the butter, which should foam beautifully in the pan. Add the sliced shallot and garlic and give the juices a stir to release any browned bits and coat the alliums in butter. Put the pan in the oven to cook for 12–15 minutes.

Take the pot out of the oven and put the chicken on a warm plate covered with foil to rest and keep warm.

Put the pan with the shallots back on the hob, pour in the reduced stock (should be around 150ml) and bring to the boil. Add the tarragon leaves and then the vegetables in order of cooking time – first the French beans and any chard stems – cook for a minute or two; then the broccoli and cabbage – cook for another minute or two; and finally the beet tops and

the peas, which should take 2 minutes more (if the peas are not very tender new ones, add them with the broccoli). If the pan has a lid, keep the vegetables covered, or use foil to seal and steam the veg inside. Keep checking, muddling them around gently and removing them as soon as they are just tender and still have their greenness – too long and they will lose vibrancy. Season if needed with salt and pepper.

Serve out the vegetables on to hot plates or a large serving dish. Pile the chicken pieces on top. Pour any chicken juices produced while resting back into the stock, boil hard to reduce for a few seconds more, then add the remaining butter and whisk around. Check the seasoning and pour over the chicken and veg to serve. Taste and squeeze over a little lemon juice if you will. Eat with tender, halved new potatoes.

GATHER COOK FEAST

Two Ways with New Potatoes

SERVES 4

Boil 500g of scrubbed new potatoes in salted water until tender –
around 20 minutes. Drain and let them steam dry for a couple of minutes,
then cut into bite-sized chunks. Now follow one of these two recipes.

With Fennel Flowers & Orange

Succulent new potatoes with creamy fennel and zest of orange.

Gently mix the potatoes with 1 tablespoon of white wine vinegar, and
the grated zest and juice of ½ an orange. Mix in 2 trimmed and finely
sliced spring onions, a good dollop of crème fraîche, and salt and pepper
to taste. Finally snip in little flowers from 5 sprays of fennel, leaving the
tiniest stem on each. Gently mix and serve warm.

With Wet Garlic & Lovage

Earthy lovage combines beautifully with new-season wet garlic and
potatoes. If the garlic is very new, it only needs the outer skin peeled
off to slice through the entire bulb, embryonic cloves and all. If the
inner skins of each clove have formed any papery quality, peel them
in the usual way and slice finely.

Heat 3 tablespoons of olive oil in a pan over a low to medium heat
and soften one finely sliced bulb of wet garlic – do not allow it to take
colour. Add the potatoes and toss to coat with the garlicky oil. Add 3
tablespoons of cider vinegar and let it bubble up around the potatoes.
Toss a couple more times, then tip into a bowl with all the pan juices.
Taste to season with salt and pepper if needed. Mix through a few
leaves of finely shredded lovage, and serve warm.

Peas, Mint & Feta

SERVES 1

A fine bowl of freshly podded peas speaks of patience and generosity –
combine with mint and Feta for a juicy supper bowl or side dish (sssh …
sometimes made too with frozen).

In boiling salted water cook 250g of podded peas until tender. Drain,
then combine in a bowl with a few finely snipped fresh mint leaves,
a good crumbling of salty Feta (80–100g), a dribble or two of good,
peppery olive oil, and flaky sea salt and black pepper.

Nasturtium Butter

MAKES A SMALL POT

Inspired by a version from Chez Panisse, melt a knob or two of this
bright, peppery butter over grilled steak, fish or boiled new potatoes.

Finely grate the zest of an unwaxed lemon over 125g of butter and
leave to soften at room temperature. Then squeeze the lemon into
a bowl. Mix a peeled and finely diced small round shallot with the
squeezed lemon juice and 1 teaspoon of red wine vinegar and leave
to macerate for an hour or so. Then drain the liquid off and keep.

Mix the shallot and around 40 finely chopped nasturtium flowers into
the lemon-zested softened butter. Add salt and crushed pink peppercorns
to taste. Now add some of the reserved shallot liquid, a teaspoon at a
time, until the butter develops a pleasing bright acidity. You will not need
it all. Pack the butter into a ramekin or small bowl, cover and chill in
the fridge, where it will keep for a week or two.

Raspberry &
Brioche Pudding

SERVES 4

2 large brioche buns or croissants –
    ideally a few days old
1½ vanilla pods
600ml full cream milk
80g white granulated sugar
3 large eggs
a pinch of sea salt
100ml double cream
a knob of butter
120g fresh raspberries, plus
    extra to serve

JUNE TO AUGUST IF USING
SUMMER RASPBERRIES

A light, soft summer bread and butter pudding made more indulgent by using sweet brioche or croissants instead of buttered bread. The raspberries become fruity little bursts of flavour among the creaminess of the intermingled custard and bread.

My local shop often gives me out-of-date croissants or brioche buns and it's these old ones that are ideal for this pudding.

This recipe can be made ahead, even the day before, and baked in time to serve. Thickly slice cold leftovers, melt butter in a hot pan and brown, to serve with poached or fresh summer fruit and a little cream.

Heat the oven to 190°C/170°C fan/gas 5.

If the brioche or croissants are fresh, lay them, split in half, on a baking tray and toast in the oven until the surfaces are crisp but there is still a little give in the middle (around 5–10 minutes). Check and remove any hard parts, then allow to cool.

Scrape the seeds out of the vanilla pods and add them with the pods to the milk and sugar in a saucepan. Bring to a bare simmer, then turn off the heat and leave to infuse until lukewarm. Remove the pods, giving them a final squeeze into the milk (for a maximum vanilla flavour).

Whisk the eggs with a pinch of salt in a large bowl until well combined, then whisk in the infused milk and the cream.

Find a deep-ish gratin dish (minimum 5cm deep) that will hold around 1 litre of liquid (you can test the volume by filling with water and measuring). Generously butter around all the edges.

Tear the brioche or croissants into bite-sized pieces, tucking them around each other to fill the dish. Don't pack the dish too full of bread or the pudding will be dry, and leave generous gaps for the custard. Sprinkle in the raspberries, tucking them between the bread.

Pour over the custard to fill the dish and leave to soak for 10–15 minutes. You may not be able to get it all in at first, but after some minutes the bread will have absorbed more of the custard and you should eventually be able to add it all. At this point you could store the assembled pudding overnight in the fridge for cooking the next day (add 30 minutes to the cooking time if it goes into the oven cold).

Cover the dish loosely with foil and place it on a baking tray. Bake for around an hour, until the custard has just set, removing the foil for the last 5 minutes or so. The middle will be the last part to cook (don't worry if it's still a little too wobbly, as it will continue cooking out of the oven). It will hold together better if you let it cool for 10–15 minutes before cutting.

Serve just warm, with thin cream, if you like, and a few more fresh raspberries.

GATHER COOK FEAST

Sweet, Rich, Shortcrust Pastry

200g plain flour
50g caster sugar
a pinch of salt
120g butter, chopped into
    small cubes
1 egg yolk
1 tablespoon cider vinegar
ice-cold water
1 whole egg, beaten

There is nothing worse than a flabby, saggy pastry bottom. To avoid this I have three breakthroughs to share – first, a thorough pre-cooking of the base, followed by an egg coating; second, the discovery of a new heavy tin with holes and a removeable base, sold as for crusty-bottomed quiches – it's brilliant; lastly, trimming your pastry case after the first baking avoids any shrinkage. Go forth and make foolproof pastry bases.

Put the dry ingredients into a bowl and rub in the butter with your thumbs and fingertips until the mixture resembles breadcrumbs. With a fork, roughly mix the egg yolk with the vinegar and add to the mixture, combining until it starts to clump together. Much water may not be needed, so dribble in ice-cold water teaspoon by teaspoon and work it until you can just form the mixture into a ball. Form the pastry into a flat bun shape, wrap in clingfilm and chill in the fridge for at least an hour.

Heat the oven to 200°C/180°C fan/gas 6.

Remove the pastry from the fridge and roll out on a floured board to a circle at least 5cm larger than you need to fill your tin. Line the tin with the pastry, easing the surplus into the corners but taking care not to stretch the pastry as you fit it in. Leave the surplus overhanging the sides and give the sides a little squeeze all around to make sure they don't collapse into the middle during baking. Prick the base a few times with a fork, and line with a big square of baking paper (big enough to overlap and protect the sides), gently eased into the base and weighted with some dry white butter beans, rice or similar. Put it back into the fridge for 15–20 minutes.

Cook the case in the oven for 15 minutes, then carefully remove the paper and beans and pop the tin back into the oven for a further 5 minutes, until the base is cooked to a delicate palest brown. Remove from the oven, trim the edges with a sharp knife, and, while still warm, brush the base with beaten egg to seal and leave to cool completely.

GATHER COOK FEAST

Gooseberry & Fennel Pie

MAKES A 23CM PIE,
SERVING 6 PEOPLE

1 pastry case (see page 147)

The filling
a handful of fennel fronds
1½ teaspoons fennel seeds
150ml full cream milk
200g gooseberries
3 tablespoons sugar
a pinch of sea salt
150g crème fraîche
4 egg yolks, plus 1 whole egg,
    beaten together until smooth

MAY TO JUNE FOR GOOSEBERRIES

Oh, the much-maligned gooseberry, hairy, mouth-puckeringly sour, green and lurking under viciously spiky branches! They are delicious, their little marbled bodies like tiny pale green watermelons and a fresh, fruity intensity unlike anything else.

Here they are combined with fennel fronds and seeds in a soft custardy pie. Fennel, although mostly used in savoury dishes, has a surprising sweetness. If you can't find fresh fennel fronds, use double the fennel seeds.

This is the first of two soft custardy pies for high summer. They share the same simple sweet pastry case. The bases can be made ahead of time but the pies are best just warm.

Make the pastry case following the method on page 147. Infuse the fennel fronds and seeds in a pan with the milk. Bring the mixture to just under the boil, then remove from the heat and leave to steep, covered, for at least 30 minutes.

Put the gooseberries, sugar and pinch of salt into a pan and cook over a medium heat for 15–20 minutes, until soft and slightly reduced. Taste the gooseberries for sweetness and add a little more sugar if you like. Some gooseberries are much tarter than others (it depends on ripeness), but try to keep the essential sharp pungency. Once you drain off any surplus water, you should end up with around 100ml of mixture. If you object to seediness the mixture can be pushed through a sieve. Mash it up a little with a fork.

Heat (or adjust if you have just made the pastry case) the oven to 190°C/170°C fan/gas 5. Remove the fennel fronds from the pan of milk and squeeze out all the delicious sweetness. Add the gooseberry mixture, crème fraîche, beaten egg yolks and whole egg. Give it a good whisk to ensure it is well mixed. The mixture should be around 500–550ml in volume – this will fill a 23 x 3cm tin, but if you have a deeper tin, add a little more crème fraîche, plus possibly an extra egg yolk, to fill it to the brim. Pour the mixture carefully into the cold pastry case and bake in the oven again for 25–30 minutes, until the pie is just starting to brown in spots on the top. It won't be set completely – that will happen once it's cool – but it should have a wobbly integrity that will give you confidence to remove it.

GATHER COOK FEAST

Camomile Pie

MAKES A 23CM PIE,
SERVING 6 PEOPLE

1 pastry case (see page 147)

The filling
5 super-fresh camomile
    tea bags or 8g loose dried
    camomile flowers
200ml full cream milk
a pinch of sea salt
1 vanilla pod, split
250ml double cream
65g caster sugar
4 egg yolks, plus 1 whole egg,
    beaten together until smooth

This pie has the dusty fragrance of camomile combined with vanilla, a perfect expression of summer. Even camomile deniers may be converted.

In this version I have used double cream, rather than crème fraîche, to balance the delicacy of camomile. If you can find them, fragrant loose dried camomile flowers are the best choice, but the freshest camomile tea bags can substitute.

You can make the pastry ahead of time, but the pie is best eaten at the precise moment it achieves lukewarm temperature. Although as I write I am enjoying a cool slice with a cup of milky coffee, which is still very good. For the time-poor or pastry-averse, pour the mixture into little ramekins for individual camomile custard pots. This pie needs nothing to go with it except perhaps a few perfectly ripe summer berries.

Make the pastry case following the method on page 147. Infuse the camomile with the milk, the pinch of salt and the vanilla pod in a lidded pan. Bring the mixture to just under the boil, then remove from the heat and leave to steep, covered, for at least 30 minutes.

Heat (or adjust if you have just made the pastry case) the oven to 190°C/170°C fan/gas 5. Make the custard. Remove the camomile and vanilla from the milk (straining if using loose camomile) and squeeze out all the delicious flavour. Put the camomile milk back into the pan with the cream, sugar and beaten eggs. Scrape the seeds from the vanilla pod and mix them back into the custard with everything else. Give it all a good whisk to make sure everything is thoroughly combined.

You should have approximately 550ml of mixture, which will fill a 23 x 3cm pastry case to the top. If your tin is deeper than the one specified, you could add a little more cream and possibly another egg yolk to make sure your dish is filled to the brim. Once you have checked, pour the mixture into the pastry case.

Bake in the oven for 25–30 minutes, until the pie is just starting to brown in spots on the top. It won't be set completely, that will happen once cooling, but it should have a wobbly integrity which will give you confidence to remove it.

Strawberry & Balsamic Vinegar Ice Cream

MAKES 6–8 SCOOPS

300g perfectly ripe strawberries, hulled and roughly chopped

100g, plus 2 tablespoons white granulated sugar

300ml double cream

a pinch of sea salt

4 egg yolks

100ml balsamic vinegar

JUNE & JULY FOR SUMMER STRAWBERRIES

It's a surprising quality of strawberries that they combine so well with savoury flavours – black pepper or balsamic vinegar – but they do. The combination works tremendously in a creamy rich ice cream, where the aromatic summer strawberries are brought into unexpected full flavour by the vinegar.

There is no need for an expensive balsamic for this recipe – a standard thin one will do, reduced down to syrupy beauty in a pan.

Mix the chopped strawberries with 2 tablespoons of sugar and leave to macerate until juicy. Heat the cream in a small saucepan with 100g of sugar and a pinch of salt until the sugar dissolves and the cream almost comes to the boil. Remove from the heat.

In a bowl, whisk the egg yolks until a little paler and smooth. Whisk in the hot cream, then return to the saucepan. Cook over a low to medium heat, stirring all the time, until the custard thickens enough to coat the back of a spoon. Take care not to let the mixture get too hot or it will curdle. Pour the custard through a sieve into a bowl and leave to cool. Give it an occasional whisk so that it cools evenly.

Boil the balsamic vinegar in a little pan until it has somewhat reduced and is starting to look quite syrupy (each vinegar will be different from another – one more acidic, another thicker – so it may reach this state when reduced by just under half or just over half but you should be left with around 45–60ml). Keep a close eye on the pan, swirling it around frequently, as it's easy to accidentally go too far. Let it cool. Blitz the strawberries to a purée, using a blender, an immersion blender or a fork and a strong arm.

When the custard has cooled, stir in the strawberry purée and enough of the reduced balsamic vinegar to be noticeable when tasted, without the mix becoming too acidic. You may well want to use it all. Remember that flavours become somewhat dulled after freezing – so make sure the flavour is punchy. Churn the mixture in your ice cream maker according to the manufacturer's instructions, then transfer to a lidded tub and freeze until firm. (See page 112 for making ice cream without an ice cream maker.)

Rose Icing Sugar

Use rose icing sugar to sweeten summer raspberries or strawberries, or use a teaspoon to make a rose cocktail with gin, a squeeze of lemon, a drop or two of rose water, sparkling water with ice and rose petals. Make this on a dry day when the roses are free from damp or dew.

Take a dry clean jar and one fragrant rose per 100g of icing sugar. Strip off the petals and make sure to remove all bugs. Then, layer by layer, build up the icing sugar interleaved with rose petals. Seal up the jar and leave for a couple of weeks, until the rose petals have gone brown and the sugar smells fragrantly of roses. Remove the rose petals, if you like, and seal up again. It's best used before the end of the summer.

Rose Macaroons

MAKES ABOUT 30 TINY
MACAROONS

50g porridge oats
3 egg whites
a pinch of salt
180g rose icing sugar (see
    page 155) or normal icing sugar
½ teaspoon lemon juice
1 teaspoon rose water
250g ground almonds

Imagine eating roses – the decadence!

These are rough little things. The pillowy oatmeal adds a cleaner note to offset the richness of the almond and the heady fragrance of the rose.

They are easy and quick to make. The rose icing sugar is a slightly indulgent but easy and lovely thing to do, but as an alternative, rose water with icing sugar will also work.

Heat the oven to 140°C/120°C fan/gas 1. Cover a baking tray with baking parchment.

Prepare all the ingredients, weighed and ready in advance of whisking the egg whites, to make sure you catch the whites at peak fluff. Blitz the oats in a food processor to a rough flour consistency. Then whisk the egg whites with the salt until they are dry and stiff. Add the sugar gradually, until the mixture has a marshmallow consistency.

Add the lemon juice and rose water (tasting carefully, as it is easy to overdo rose water). Finally fold in the almonds and blitzed oats carefully.

Using two teaspoons, spoon out on to the baking tray, little mound by little mound. Each one should be around the size of a walnut.

Cook in the oven for 40–55 minutes, until they are firm and starting to colour a little around the edges, but still chewy inside. Cool them fully on a rack before eating, perhaps with a cup of an astringent milk-less China tea, to savour the flavour.

GATHER COOK FEAST

Lavender Cake

25–30 stalks of lavender,
    depending on size
250g unsalted butter,
    at room temperature
200g caster sugar
a pinch of sea salt
3 large eggs
300g self-raising flour, sieved
2 teaspoons lemon juice
½ teaspoon vanilla extract
70ml milk

The icing
100g icing sugar, sieved
1¼ tablespoons lemon juice
a few lavender buds

MID-SUMMER FOR LAVENDER

Put away any thoughts of lavender being limited to the linen drawer. Here is a simple cake softly and dustily fragrant with the nectar that drives bees wild, each honeyed nibble reminiscent of a drowsy flowerbed loud with bees.

Freshly gathered lavender buds are easily dried in the oven and only take a few minutes to prepare. Ready-dried lavender is commonly available – see page 335 for sources, or try your local wholefood store.

The degree of perfume will vary depending on the source and quality of lavender. If you are drying lavender from full flush summer growth and potency you will need less than shop-bought dried lavender of uncertain age, and for this reason I have listed a range for the quantity of lavender required.

If you are lucky enough to have sweetly smelling lavender growing in your garden, window box or balcony, harvest roughly 25–30 flower stalks. Spread them on a baking tray and put them into a low oven (130–140°C/110–120°C fan/gas ½–1) for 5–10 minutes. Keep checking them during this time. After around 5 minutes, you will notice that the kitchen is filled with a glorious perfume. You need to find the exact moment when the heads are just drying out – the lavender will feel a tiny bit damp and waxy, but when you remove it from the oven the remaining moisture will evaporate and the heads will dry. If you leave them in the oven until they feel crisp, the fragrance will tip over into toasted and be spoilt.

Allow them to cool, then strip the buds from the stalks and chop just a little bit to an even texture – slightly less than bud size but definitely not dust – sort of half bud.

Heat the oven to 190°C/170°C fan/gas 5 and line a 20cm springform round tin with baking paper.

Cream the butter, sugar and pinch of salt together until they are light and fluffy. Add the eggs one by one, beating the mixture well to incorporate and adding a tablespoon of flour at each stage to keep the mixture smooth. Then add the lemon juice and vanilla extract.

Cut and fold in the rest of the flour using as few movements as possible. Once the flour is all incorporated, add the milk and finally the lavender (reserving a sprinkle for the icing). Use a quantity of lavender to suit your taste.

Spoon the mixture evenly into the cake tin and cook in the oven for 40–55 minutes, until golden. Keep a careful eye, because ovens vary so much – the top should be golden and a skewer should come out just moist.

Allow the cake to cool well on a rack, then ice with a mixture of icing sugar and lemon juice to coat the top. Scatter lavender buds on the still-wet icing and leave to set before serving with a cup of Earl Grey tea or some summer berries and a little cream.

Elderflower Cordial

MAKES AROUND 3–4 BOTTLES

30 perfect wide sprays of
   elderflowers (add a few more
   if the heads are small)
1.5 litres water
900g white granulated sugar
3 unwaxed lemons

MAY TO JUNE FOR ELDERFLOWERS

On a warm summer morning, collecting enough elderflowers to make a batch of cordial is not a great trial. The blooms are best picked early in the day, as soon as the sun has dried out the heads. Take a walking stick or umbrella to help you carefully pull down the branches to reach the best sprays, high up in the sunshine. As usual, avoid bushes alongside heavy traffic or sprayed fields, where the blooms may be tainted.

This way of preparing the cordial stresses the flowers as little as possible – gently extracting all the heady and delicate woodsy flavours of the elderflowers. Citric acid is often added to elderflower cordial as a preservative, but I find it drowns out the fragrance of the flowers, so this recipe uses lemon instead of citric acid to provide the acidity needed, and the freezer will serve to keep the cordial through the flowerless parts of the year if you need it to.

Drink the cordial on its own with ice and sparkling water; or use it to flavour gooseberries; or as a mixer with gin or champagne.

Shake all the insects off the sprays of elderflowers. Snip off most of the stalk as close to the head as possible. Throw the stalks away.

Boil the water and pour over the sugar in a big heatproof bowl. Stir to dissolve. Zest the lemons using a lemon zester, then juice them and add the juice and zest to the sugar syrup. Allow the mixture to cool, then immerse all the flower heads, stirring to fully wet and submerge them. Cover with a tea towel and leave in a cool place overnight to steep. The next day, sterilize three or four bottles (instructions for sterilizing are on page 105).

Strain the cordial through damp muslin into the sterilized bottles (you may find it easier to decant it into a jug first) or into clean, labelled plastic bags or bottles for the freezer. Bottled elderflower cordial should keep in the fridge for around 4 weeks. Frozen cordial will last until the next year – but once defrosted, use within a couple of weeks. Freeze the cordial in smaller quantities to use in recipes through the year. It is quite delicious added to some gooseberries in a pan with a little sugar, then reduced over a low heat for 30 minutes or so to make a dark, pink-y compote to add to yoghurt or porridge.

RIPE GOLDEN
HEDGEROW **FIELD**
& PASTURE BEEF
GRAZE TILTH EARTH
ROOTS SLOPE UMBER
HORSERADISH

BEANS LATE BAKED
SOURDOUGH MALT
FURROWS RABBITS
HARVEST BARLEY

Almost all landscapes, however 'natural' they may at first appear, are the product of human interventions, over decades, centuries and even millennia. Farmland represents the fundamental example of interaction between humankind and the natural landscape, changed and adapted by layers of human culture and practice since Neolithic times and, more recently, by scientific and technological innovation as farmers have sought to feed a growing population. Modern society and agriculture are inextricably linked – we cannot have the first without the second.

These often beautiful but created landscapes can reconnect us with our own cultural history and traditions as well as bringing an appreciation of the labours of those who are out in all weathers, in often dangerous and uncomfortable conditions, to bring our bread to the table and our beer to the glass. Not all is bucolic, but thinking more deeply about the means of food production can help us understand and inform the food journey.

For this chapter, we surrounded ourselves with expansive ideas of harvest: of forgotten (but newly rediscovered) beans and grains; of fields of root vegetables; of sturdy beef cattle grazing rich pasture. Rabbits too, which we imagined running and jinking through fields of freshly mown stubble in late summer. We rolled and kneaded and stirred, thinking of acres of ripe grain. We scrambled through brambles for berries and nuts and we borrowed from other cultures to reinvent – for our own landscape – meals that could have been made by our ancestors.

I challenge anyone not to be moved by a field of ripe or near-ripe barley, the beauty of the whiskered seed heads rippling and shivering in the lightest breeze. Its taste is both rugged and starchy, with a succulent quality and a flavour that can even hint at honey. It will grow almost anywhere and, in its wholegrain incarnation, is nutritious and fully deserves wider use. It is a quintessential autumn taste, being inextricably associated with the malting process, where the grain is wetted, sprouted, then finally roasted – a process that releases sugars and starches in degrees of nutty and bitter-sweet flavours as a precursor to brewing beer, but also to produce the sticky, brown malt extract.

The produce of our farmland is rich and varied, with a long and celebrated history of quality beef, dairy and grain production. This heritage is now being reinvigorated by a growing band of dedicated farmers and producers who favour rare breeds, old varieties and less intensive production methods. I applaud their efforts too, and list some of them at the back of the book.

Whole Grain Barley Porridge

SERVES 1

The basic recipe
50g whole barley grains
boiling water
150–250ml milk
a pinch of sea salt

Over the years I have variously eaten: a savoury olive-oil-based gruel in the deserts of Morocco, buckwheat and millet porridge in Tanzania, rice porridge in Japan topped with miso and fermented fish guts, oatmeal in the US, and many versions of Scottish porridge oats in my own home, made by my porridge-talented husband, Jamie – a whole world of nutritious breakfast complexity using various grains.

This recipe is for whole barley grains. For a less sturdy version you may choose to use a pearl barley, which would cook slightly more quickly, but will have had some of its fibre (and the nutritious endosperm) stripped away by the polishing process.

You can use other grains too – farro, freekeh, rice, spelt and even wheat grains – but there may be a slight variation in cooking times. Wheat grains take around 5–10 minutes more to cook, farro a tiny bit less. Keep an eye on the pan and taste to see when the grains are tender.

Here I have provided a basic recipe with a number of finishing options, including a savoury one. Once you get into the swing of it, many permutations are possible. Times here are for a just-tender result – for a softer finish, add 5–10 minutes.

Put the grains into a good heavy pan and cover with three times their volume of boiling water. Leave to steep until the water is cool, then cover and refrigerate overnight.

In the morning, pour off the water, add 150ml of milk and a pinch of salt and bring to the boil, simmering on a gentle heat for 20–25 minutes. Add more milk during the cooking to ensure the grains are soft, moist and slipping around in a glorious milky sludge. The amount of milk needed will depend on the type of grains you use and how much water the grains have absorbed overnight, so keep a close eye and add a little more occasionally to keep it moist as it bubbles away.

Choose from the list opposite to finish off the porridge.

The first in each list of ingredients should be added to the porridge after 15 minutes and cooked together with the grains for the last 5 minutes, stirring occasionally. When the grains are chewily tender, take the pan off the heat and pour into a bowl. Then add the appropriate toppings.

— Add a handful of mixed raisins and toasted flaked almonds to the pan and top with cream and brown sugar.

— Add 2 tablespoons of coconut milk and a small handful of raisins to the pan and top with plain yoghurt, toasted coconut flakes and a few raspberries.

— Add half a chopped pear and a tiny pinch of saffron to the pan and top with plain yoghurt and honey.

— Add a small handful of chopped almonds and a teaspoon of honey to the pan and top with blackberries or blueberries and plain yoghurt.

— Add chopped dried figs to the pan and top with plain yoghurt, a sprinkle of brown sugar and some toasted sesame seeds.

— Add 1 or 2 teaspoons of sweet miso to the pan and top with a soft (or hard) boiled egg, half a chopped avocado and a little chopped parsley.

Spicy Breakfast Peas

SERVES 6 FOR A
HEARTY SUNDAY BRUNCH

400g whole dried Carlin peas

4 tablespoons sunflower or olive oil

a large knob of butter

2 red onions, peeled and finely diced

2 fat cloves of garlic, peeled
    and very finely chopped

3 tablespoons spice mix (see below)

3 tablespoons tomato purée

sea salt and black pepper

The topping

9 cherry tomatoes, quartered

2 large medium-hot green chillies,
    deseeded and chopped

6 eggs, hard-boiled, peeled
    and cut into wedges

plain yoghurt

flaky sea salt

extra virgin olive oil

The spice mix

2 teaspoons fenugreek seeds

1 teaspoon coriander seeds

1 teaspoon cumin seeds

1 teaspoon black cardamom seeds
    (or green cardamom seeds)

1 teaspoon allspice berries

1 teaspoon black peppercorns

4 cloves

2 teaspoons paprika

2 teaspoons chilli powder

2 teaspoons ground ginger

1 teaspoon dried thyme or oregano

This is a rich, very spicy breakfast dish for a slow Sunday morning, which will drive out any morning-after muddiness with its chilli kick. I love the idea of having more savoury breakfast options.

I like the Black Badger variety of Carlin pea but you can substitute other varieties, chickpeas, or many other dried beans. Peas and beans can take a variable length of time to cook; it depends on variety and age. This dish is better made in advance but it will keep for up to 5 days in the fridge, so a big batch could serve various meals.

These peas are really quite spicy – which is the point – but if your taste is for less chilli, adjust as you like. Toppings are suggested, but also try them with a fried or poached egg. Less British, but also delicious, could be a ripe, sliced avocado. Or grate some sharp Cheddar over with sour cream. Or add some zingy, green salad leaves and eat for supper.

Lightly toast the whole spices in a small dry frying pan until fragrant, then grind them to a powder in an electric spice grinder or with a mortar and pestle. Mix with the paprika, chilli powder, ginger and thyme. This makes more than you need. Store the surplus in a jar out of direct light.

Soak the dried peas in three times their volume of cold water overnight. Drain and rinse the peas, then place in a saucepan with enough cold water to cover by a good 2.5cm. Cover and simmer for around an hour, until the peas are tender but still holding their shape (if they are taking longer than this, add ½ teaspoon of bicarbonate of soda to speed them up).

Heat the oil and butter in a medium-sized heavy-based pot. Add most of the diced onion, keeping back around 3 tablespoons to use raw on top. Soften over a medium heat for around 10 minutes. Add the garlic and soften for another 5 minutes, until both alliums are just starting to caramelize. Add the spice mix and stir for a minute, then add the tomato purée and stir for a further couple of minutes.

Use a slotted spoon to transfer the cooked peas to the onion-spice mixture, then pour over enough of the pea water to just cover. Season with a very generous pinch of salt. Bring everything to the boil, then reduce to a low simmer, cover and cook until the flavours all come together and the peas are starting to fall apart (about 30 minutes).

Mash a few of the peas to help create a rich sauce, adding more water if the dish seems dry. Check the seasoning.

Divide the peas between bowls and arrange with little piles of tomato, chilli, red onion and boiled egg on each. Give each a dollop of yoghurt, season the tomatoes and egg with flaky salt and dribble a little extra virgin olive oil over the top.

Lentil, Green Peppercorn &
Salt-Baked Vegetable Warm Salad

SERVES 4 AS A LUNCH OR
SUPPER, 6 AS A SIDE DISH

8 small skinny carrots, with tops
4 small turnips, with tops
8 small beets, with tops
800g–1kg basic table salt, for
    salt-baking (see page 187)
250g mixed brown and/or Puy lentils
a small glug of olive oil
1 bay leaf, fresh or dried
1 clove of garlic, peeled and left whole
2 tablespoons green peppercorns
    in brine, lightly chopped
1 tablespoon white sesame seeds,
    lightly toasted
25g chives, chopped

The dressing
1 tablespoon elderberry, damson
    or raspberry vinegar
1 tablespoon red wine vinegar
4 tablespoons good olive oil
sea salt and black pepper

This deep and dark autumnal salad scattered with glistening shards of salt-baked vegetables is a satisfying dish for a homely supper or lunch. Salt-baking intensifies and brings out the savour of each root, locking in inherent moisture. A fruity vinegar adds a complex, sweet note to counter the earthy flavours. Find the elderberry vinegar recipe on page 259, or buy a raspberry or damson version instead (see sources, page 334). If you can't find a fruit vinegar, replace with a good balsamic vinegar.

You can use either brown lentils or Puy, or even combine both, to use up annoying ends of boxes on the shelves.

Prepare and salt-bake the vegetables as directed on page 187 – leaving a little stalk if you like. While the vegetables are baking, cook the lentils. Rinse in a sieve under cold running water, then put them into a pan, together with a small glug of olive oil, the bay leaf and the garlic. Add cold water to a depth of 2cm above the surface of the lentils. Do not salt the water at the beginning because this can inhibit cooking.

Bring to a rapid boil, then reduce the heat until simmering bubbles are just breaking the surface. Keep an eye on the water level, and if the pan begins to dry out add a little more boiling water to keep the level of water just above the lentils. Check for tenderness after 15 minutes and add salt to taste. Depending on the age of the lentils they can take up to 30 minutes to become tender. When they are just tender, drain off any surplus water through a sieve and pop the sieve back over the pan with the lid on to keep the lentils warm and dry.

Whisk the dressing ingredients with a fork, in a cup or small bowl, ready for the salad assembly. Taste to make sure the balance is as you'd like and adjust the elements accordingly. To assemble the dish, put the lentils into a big, wide bowl. Riddle the chopped green peppercorns and the toasted sesame seeds through the lentils, distributing them evenly. Mix in half the dressing. Take the salt-baked vegetables and slice lengthways into big, long shards, exposing the glistening interiors of the roots. It's important the vegetables are big and bold, to offset the tiny scale of the lentils. Tuck the pieces in and around the lentils. Scatter with the chopped chives and the remaining dressing and serve while still warm.

Braised Short Ribs with Polenta & Horseradish

SERVES 6

1.75kg beef short ribs, cut into 4cm-
    wide strips across the rack
sea salt and black pepper
a dash of olive oil
2 large red onions,
    peeled and chopped
2 carrots, peeled and chopped
3 sticks of celery, chopped
8 cloves of garlic, peeled
    and left whole
2 small dried chillies
2 sprigs of fresh rosemary
2 fresh bay leaves
5 or 6 fresh thyme sprigs
4 big, but fine, pared strips
    of orange zest
2 tablespoons tomato purée
2 rounded teaspoons brown sugar
1 bottle of red wine
1 litre beef or veal stock
a good handful of small, pitted
    black or violet olives

The polenta
1 litre vegetable or chicken stock
1 litre milk
350g coarse-ground polenta
40g finely grated Parmesan
80g butter

The gremolata
6 sprigs of fresh tarragon
2 tablespoons finely grated fresh
    horseradish root
1 lemon, ready to zest

As the air cools, leaves fall, and daylight fades, the urge to braise a piece of meat to fragrant softness grows.

Persuade your butcher to cut the short ribs across the rack rather than along the bone. Each strip should be around 4cm wide, 15–20cm long, and contain three or four small cross-sections of rib bone. Avoid quick-cook polenta here in favour of the slower, creamier qualities of coarse-ground polenta cooked for a long time. If you search you can find this in many places, often masquerading as coarse-ground cornmeal. It's the same thing. The addition of a punchy gremolata on the side counters any suspicion of over-richness with frisky mouthfuls of lemon, tarragon and horseradish.

Time is the unstated ingredient here. Time to make the polenta well. Time to allow the short ribs to braise to melting softness, and time after cooking for the braise to mature and the flavours to combine and meld together. So, if you can, cook the ribs the day before. There should be plenty of polenta to go around and some for lunch the day afterwards too.

Heat the oven to 180°C/160°C fan/gas 4 and season the meat all over with salt and pepper.

Put a dash of olive oil into a wide frying pan and heat until shimmering. Brown the meat on all sides over a high heat, then arrange in a single layer in a big ovenproof dish.

Add the onions, carrots, celery and garlic to the oil left in the frying pan and soften over a medium-high heat, stirring frequently, for 5 minutes. Add the chillies, rosemary, bay leaves, thyme and orange zest, stirring for another 5 minutes until the vegetables are starting to soften and colour and everything smells amazing.

Stir in the tomato purée, then add the brown sugar and wine and let it bubble and reduce by half – about 10 minutes more. Add the stock and bring to a rolling boil, then pour everything over the short ribs. Arrange the short ribs so that their meaty parts are submerged and only the bones are protruding. Cover with foil and place in the oven for around 2 hours, until the meat is really tender. Check on them after half an hour – the liquid should be very gently simmering. If it is bubbling too rapidly,

AUTUMN TO WINTER FOR HORSE-
RADISH, WHICH NEEDS COOLING
SOIL TO DEVELOP PUNGENCY

reduce the oven temperature or lift up a corner of the foil. While the meat is cooking, make the polenta. Bring the stock and milk to the boil in a large pot and season with salt. Add the polenta, whisking vigorously while the mixture comes back to the boil. When it starts to thicken, switch to a wooden spoon or spatula and reduce the heat to low.

Continue cooking for around 45 minutes, stirring occasionally to check it isn't catching on the bottom; add a little hot water from the kettle if it feels too stiff. Finally stir in the Parmesan, butter and more salt and pepper to taste. Keep warm over a very low heat.

When the meat is done, lift it out on to a board and divide each strip into two or three pieces. Strain the braising liquid through a sieve into a large saucepan, pressing down on the vegetables to extract as much juice as possible (the vegetables are finished with now). Skim the fat off the top of the sauce, then briskly boil to reduce by around half, until intensely flavoured and thickened – about 10–15 minutes. Add the meat back to the sauce along with the olives and bring everything back to a gentle simmering bubble. Taste and season.

Make the gremolata shortly before serving. Remove the tarragon leaves from the stalks and chop finely. Put them into a bowl with the finely grated horseradish. Take the lemon and pare off six paper-thin strips. Chop these strips very finely, into the tiniest dice possible, and mix really well with the tarragon and horseradish. These tiny chunks give more lemony intensity than grated or zested rind, but you will choose.

To serve, divide the polenta between warmed shallow bowls. Place the meat on top and pour plenty of sauce over and around. Scatter the horseradish gremolata over the ribs and serve immediately.

Toasted Hay Mashed Potatoes

Mashed potatoes get a sweet-nutty makeover using toasted hay infused rapeseed oil.

Heat the oven to 190°C/170°C fan/gas 5. Spread a good large handful of sweet meadow hay on a baking tray and bake for 40 minutes, until dry and fragrantly toasted. Pack the hay into a jar and cover with rapeseed oil. Leave for 24–48 hours to steep and for the flavour to infuse into the oil. Use the oil to mash tender boiled potatoes. Season with salt and pepper to taste.

Whole Roast Cauliflower

SERVES 2

Creamy white curds of cauliflower fringed by green are roasted to amber and served with a tahini sauce. It only needs a good salad alongside for an easy, light supper.

Heat the oven to 220°C/200°C fan/gas 7.

Take a smallish cauliflower of around 800–900g. Remove the biggest, coarsest leaves and the stub of the stem. Split it vertically down the middle – top to stem. On each of the flat sides, cut a deep V out of the stem to reduce thickness. Place the two halves, flat side down, on a baking tray and rub the curds with a good dousing of olive oil, a squeeze of lemon juice, and a very good sprinkling of flaky sea salt, black pepper and poppy seeds.

Roast in the oven until golden and tender – around 20–30 minutes. Eat with a sauce of tahini sharpened with lemon juice, loosened with a little water and well seasoned with flaky sea salt and black pepper.

GATHER COOK FEAST

Squash & Sage Speltotto

SERVES 4

1 decent-sized good tasty squash
    (around 900g), peeled, chopped
    into 2cm cubes, peelings reserved
2 tablespoons extra virgin olive oil
sea salt and black pepper
500–600ml vegetable or chicken stock
55g butter
2 banana shallots, peeled and sliced
1 clove of garlic, peeled and chopped
200g whole spelt grains (or farro),
    rinsed and drained
1 large glass of white wine
50g halved walnuts
20 fresh sage leaves
2 good big handfuls of baby spinach,
    rinsed and spun dry
100g Gubbeen, Comté or Gruyère,
    cut into 1cm cubes
a good grating of Parmesan

AUGUST TO WINTER
FOR MOST SQUASH

Squash are so very beautiful – from the once rare, but now ubiquitous, butternut squash, to the magnificent Crown Prince or the breathtaking and photogenic Blue Hokkaido or Kabocha squash, our choices are widening all the time. Choose a firm, red-fleshed variety if you can, for colour and taste in this warming recipe.

You can use spelt or farro. Cooking times would be slightly less for pearled grains.

Heat the oven to 220°C/200°C fan/gas 7.

Liberally coat the chopped squash in half the olive oil, salt and pepper and arrange on a baking sheet. Roast in the oven for 35 minutes, until soft and caramelized around the edges. While the squash is cooking, use the peelings and innards from your squash prep to enhance the stock. Boil them in the stock for 10 minutes, then sieve, ready for cooking the spelt.

Melt a knob of butter and the remaining tablespoon of olive oil in a largish pan and fry the shallots and garlic until transparent. Add the drained spelt and toss for a little while in the buttery oil. Then add the wine and simmer until reduced a little. Add the stock, keeping it topped up to just cover the spelt. Continue to simmer slowly, adding stock as needed, until the spelt is tender. While the spelt is cooking, in a small pan, fry the walnuts in a knob of butter until golden. Remove, sprinkle with a very little sea salt, and set aside. Then, adding a little more butter if needed, fry the sage leaves until crisp and drain on a wad of kitchen paper. If any butter is left over, save for pouring into the spelt at the end.

Once the spelt is al dente, stop adding stock and reduce a little until the spelt is just wet. Carefully fold in the baby spinach and allow it to wilt. Then add the squash, the cubes of cheese and some small cubes of the remaining butter (plus any melted butter). Leave with the lid on for a few moments, to allow the spinach and cheese to soften, then mix through half the walnuts and sage leaves. Check the seasoning. Then scatter the rest of the walnuts, the rest of the sage and finally the grated Parmesan on top to serve.

Rare Rib-Eye with Sweet-Sour Onions

SERVES 6

1kg beef rib-eye, in two 4cm
    thick steaks
sea salt and black pepper
olive oil

The sweet-sour onions
4 bay leaves, fresh if possible
4 good sprigs of fresh rosemary
6 medium red onions, peeled
    and cut into wedges held
    together by the root end
3 tablespoons olive oil
4 tablespoons basic balsamic vinegar
1 teaspoon sugar

The horseradish crème fraîche
around 100g fresh horseradish root
200g crème fraîche
a squeeze of lemon

To serve
peppery leaves such as watercress,
    mustard leaves or rocket

AUTUMN TO WINTER FOR HORSE-
RADISH, WHICH NEEDS COOLING
SOIL TO DEVELOP PUNGENCY

Doorsteps of juicy steak, seared and branded in a blindingly hot pan, are just asking for sweet-sour caramelized onions, a horseradish kick and some peppery leaves to play a fully satisfying food-chord. The only possible addition could be a few tiny plain boiled potatoes of good character.

The trick to this dish is insisting that the butcher cuts the beef rib-eye for you at least 4cm thick, each steak weighing 500g or more. This way you can be sure to leave a good part of the centre rare and juicy. There is no need to use an expensive balsamic for the onions (too sweet) – a cheap one will do. Instead of balsamic you could also use elderberry vinegar (see page 259).

Leftover horseradish crème fraîche will keep in the fridge for a few days, for any mackerel, smoked salmon or beef sandwich that happens along.

Generously season the steaks all over with salt and pepper, rub with a dash of oil and leave at room temperature while you prepare everything else.

Heat the oven to 220°C/200°C fan/gas 7. Choose a roasting tin or baking dish in which the onions will fit snugly and scatter the bay and rosemary on the base. Place the onions on top and pour over the oil and vinegar, then season with salt and pepper and sprinkle with the sugar. Roast for around 40 minutes until the onions are tender and starting to caramelize, turning them over once or twice during cooking.

Meanwhile peel the horseradish and grate half of it very finely. Mix this into the crème fraîche with a squeeze of lemon juice and a pinch of salt. Taste and add more grated horseradish if you like the heat. Refrigerate to thicken up.

Heat a cast-iron grill pan for 5 minutes over a high flame until it is ferociously hot. Turn on the extractor fan, open the windows and disconnect the smoke alarm, as the next bit may be smoky. Lay the steaks in the hot pan and leave them for several minutes to first develop grill marks and then release themselves from the pan. Now rotate them by 90 degrees and leave for another couple of minutes. Flip the steaks and repeat on the other side. They should be nicely browned on the outside but still very rare inside, feeling squidgy to the touch.

Remove to an oven tray and let rest for at least 15 minutes or even up to an hour.

Finally put the steaks into the oven to finish off for 10 minutes, then rest them for 10 minutes, tented with foil to keep them warm.

Slice the steaks thinly and serve immediately with the sweet-sour onions and their sticky sauce, the horseradish crème fraîche and fresh leaves.

Salt-Baked Celeriac, Beet & Turnip Pasties

MAKES 4 SMALL PASTIES OR 2 HEFTY ONES

The pastry

200g wholegrain spelt flour,
  plus extra for rolling

a good pinch of sea salt

100g cold salted butter, chopped
  into small pieces

2–3 tablespoons cold water, to mix

For salt-baking

450g mixed celeriac, beetroot
  and white turnips

2 banana shallots or 4 round shallots

4 cloves of garlic

800g–1kg basic table salt, for
  salt-baking (see page 187)

For pan-cooking
(alternative method only)

1 tablespoon olive oil

20g salted butter

1 banana shallot or 2 round shallots,
  peeled and finely sliced

2 cloves of garlic, peeled
  and very finely chopped

400g prepared mixed celeriac,
  beetroot and white turnips, peeled,
  chopped into 1cm cubes

To finish

2–3 teaspoons tamari
  (or dark soy sauce)

sea salt and black pepper

3 spring onions, tough bits
  removed, very finely sliced

40g sharp Cheddar, grated

The original portable hiking food: rough, small and tasty pasties made using salt-baked vegetables. Put warm in your pocket and eat in a bleak, windswept landscape.

Wholegrain spelt flour delivers an all-round earthy wholesomeness that my family adore, but lighter versions have their own merits: try 50:50 plain flour to wholegrain spelt or wholemeal flour as an alternative.

The method for salt-baking vegetables can be found on page 187. For a quicker prep I have added an alternative method of pan-cooking the veg. This method will get you out on the mountain around an hour earlier.

Heat the oven to 200°C/180°C fan/gas 6.

For salt-baking

Bake the root vegetables first (using the method on page 187), checking and removing the shallots and garlic as soon as they are cooked. Once all the veggies are cooked, leave the oven on to cook the pasties.

Chop off any dried tips, root ends or tough bits and roughly peel (little bits of remaining skin don't matter) the roasted veg. Peel the shallots and garlic. Chop into small pieces on a board and mash with a fork. Sprinkle the tamari over the veg, grind some black pepper over (it's unlikely you'll need salt, given where these have been for an hour or more), then add the chopped spring onions and mash roughly.

For pan-cooking (alternative method only)

Heat the olive oil and butter in a lidded frying pan over a medium heat. Gently sauté the shallot for 2–3 minutes until translucent, then add the garlic for a further minute or so. Add all the chopped vegetables and stir around until the alliums are distributed and evenly coated with the oil and butter mix. Then put the lid on and cook gently for 25–30 minutes until softened and very slightly caramelized. Keep an eye on the pan and give the veggies a stir from time to time.

When cooked, sprinkle the tamari over the veg, season with sea salt and black pepper and add the chopped spring onions. Give everything a stir again and check the seasoning.

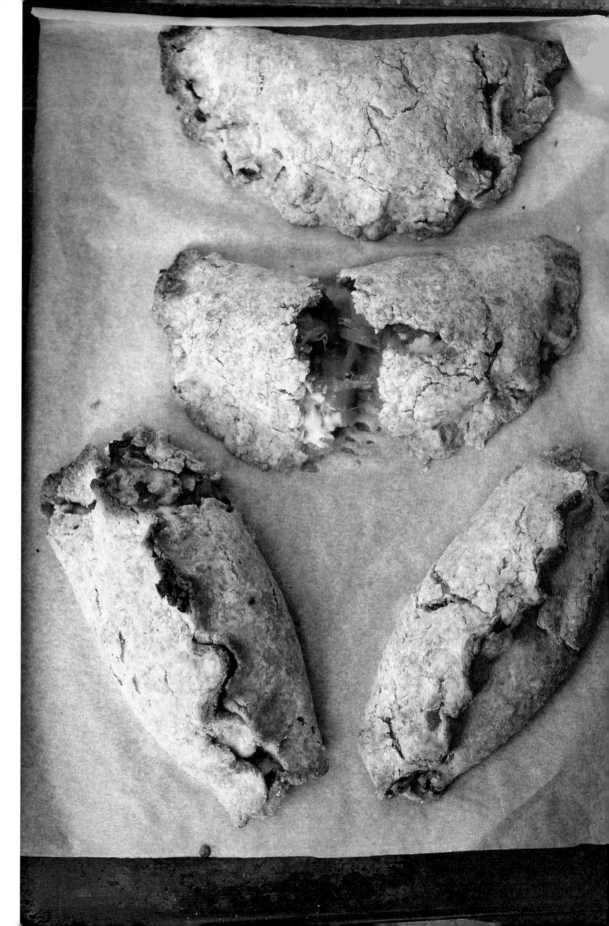

GATHER COOK FEAST

SALT-BAKED CELERIAC, BEET &
TURNIP PASTIES / CONTINUED

AUTUMN AND WINTER
FOR CELERIAC

The pastry

Put the flour, salt and butter into a bowl and rub in the butter with
your thumbs and fingertips until the mixture resembles dry breadcrumbs
(or whizz it in a food processor). Then with a fork, mix in the water,
tablespoon by tablespoon, combining until it starts to clump together
and you can form the mixture into a ball. There is no need to chill
wholemeal pastry because chilling will make it very difficult to roll.

Divide the pastry into four equal-sized pieces. Using a dusting of flour,
roll each piece out into a circle approximately 15cm in diameter.

Divide the veggie mixture into four and spoon into the centre of each of
the four rounds. Sprinkle the cheese over the veggie mixture and close up
the pasty by crimping the edges with your fingers. These are rough and
ready little beasties, so let go of perfection as you put them together.

Carefully lift the pasties on to a lined or non-stick baking tray and
place in the hot oven to bake for 30–40 minutes, until golden at the edges.
If you plan to take them on a hike, wrap them in foil and something
insulating to retain the warmth for as long as possible.

Or serve at once with a salad of crisp, interesting leaves and a dollop of
good chunky chutney.

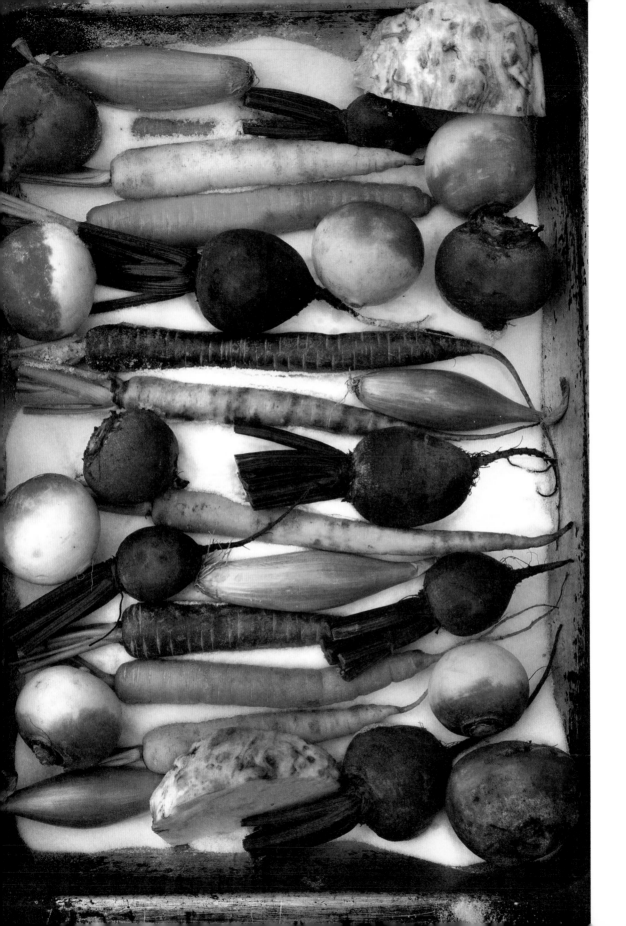

Salt-Baked Vegetables

The process of salt-baking under foil intensifies the savoury character of any root vegetable, at the same time gently moistening it with its own trapped vapours. Use any root vegetables: carrots, parsnips, turnips, swede, beetroot, celeriac or salsify. Onions, shallots and garlic can also work well.

Scrub them, dry them, cut off any damaged areas or hard tips (this is particularly important with celeriac, which always comes with a tangle of rooty areas and scabby bits) but don't peel, because the skin will act to trap all the juices and as a barrier to the salt. If your vegetables have leaves attached, leave a little of the stalk showing. Cut larger roots in half, quarters or wedges so that, as far as possible, all the veggies cook at around the same speed.

Heat the oven to 200°C/180°C fan/gas 6.

Take a roasting dish big enough to fit everything in a single layer and fill the base with a 1cm layer of basic table salt. The quantity of salt you need will depend on the size of tin and the number of veggies. As a guide, a 500g bag of salt will fill an average roasting tin.

Place all the roots evenly on the surface of the salt, skin side down, then cover the entire dish with a layer of foil, sealing the edges well.

Place the whole dish in the oven and bake for 1–1¼ hours, until the vegetables are tender. The time taken will be dependent on their size, so after around 40–45 minutes, intermittently check and remove ones that have become soft.

Allow to cool a little before peeling off the vegetables from the hardened layer of salt. Give the surfaces that have been in contact with the salt a little dusting and then use as required in a recipe or as a vegetable side dish. They are delicious with the slow roast pork on page 251, and are used in the salt-baked pasties on page 182 and the lentil, green peppercorn and salt-baked vegetable warm salad on page 171.

Savoury Tomatoes on Sourdough

SERVES 1

Flavourful late summer tomatoes softened with garlic and anchovy,
a snip of marjoram and some crumbs of frisky Feta on hot, buttered
sourdough toast.

In a small frying pan, soften 1 peeled and sliced clove of garlic in a little
olive oil. Add around 200g of the best late summer tomatoes, split into
pieces. Mash in the hot pan with 2 anchovy fillets, snipping in a few
leaves of fresh marjoram. Season with black pepper as it softens and
reduces to a rich paste.

Toast a good piece of sourdough bread. Crumble a couple of large lumps
of Feta into the tomato mixture. Liberally butter the sourdough toast with
salted butter. Spread over the tomato mixture and eat proper hot.

Braised Rabbit with Lemon & Olives

SERVES 4

1 farmed rabbit, jointed into 6
    pieces (1.2–1.4kg)
sea salt
juice of 2 lemons
2 big red onions, peeled
    and finely sliced
3 fat cloves of garlic, peeled and
    very finely chopped
1 tablespoon powdered ginger
2 teaspoons black pepper
1 teaspoon turmeric
a pinch or two of hot chilli powder
the rind from 1 large preserved
    lemon (or 2 small), rinsed
    and diced, plus extra
100g violet olives (not pitted)
100ml olive oil
a 20g bunch of fresh parsley
a 40g bunch of fresh coriander

Slow-cooked rabbit, rich with intensely savoury cooking juices, a kick of preserved lemon and speckled with beautiful violet olives, needs nothing more than a portion of simple barley couscous to complete.

Choose a farmed rabbit for this dish – it will yield more juice and tenderness more quickly than the field-gym wild one. But either is good. If using wild rabbit, plan for a longer, slower cooking time and keep it moist. For rabbit sources see page 334, or make this with chicken instead. Violet olives are available from Algerian or Moroccan shops, or substitute green.

Season the meat lightly with salt and place in a heavy-bottomed casserole pot with all the other ingredients except for the herbs. Mix with your hands and leave to marinate for up to an hour.

Separate the herb leaves from their stems and keep the leaves for finishing. Very finely chop the stems and add them to the pot.

Place the pot on a low heat, cover and simmer slowly until the rabbit is very tender and starting to come away from the bone – about 1 hour. Every now and then, use a spoon or spatula to move the meat around and turn it over, so that everything cooks evenly and nothing catches on the bottom of the pot. If the rabbit looks dry, add a glass of water.

Taste to check the seasoning, add a little more preserved lemon if you like, and serve with a scattering of the parsley and coriander leaves.

Field Fabada

SERVES 6–8

500g dried white beans

500g rindless smoked pancetta,
    in one piece

2 tablespoons olive oil

2 yellow onions, peeled
    and finely diced

2 fat cloves of garlic, peeled
    and very finely chopped

a couple of bay leaves

a couple of sprigs of fresh thyme

a couple of sprigs of fresh parsley

a good pinch of saffron threads

½ teaspoon smoked sweet paprika

2 or 3 morcilla-style blood sausages
    (around 200–250g)

2 or 3 cooking chorizos
    (around 200–250g)

sea salt and black pepper

Not many of us work in the fields nowadays, but after any day of taxing work, a fabada – a warm dish of beans from Asturias – would be a welcome, sustaining supper as autumn draws in and coats come out of the cupboard. This one is super-rich and succulent, based on the original dish, but with British beans, chorizo and blood sausage.

Fava beans have been grown in these lands since the Iron Age, and now the idea of British farmers growing local beans for drying is being revived by a young company, Hodmedod's. I love the idea that our fields could be filled, Thoreau-like, with beautiful bean plants, fragrant in flower and supplying vital extra nitrogen to the soil and pollen to our embattled insects. The ideal bean to use is the Gog Magog bean (which is actually a type of white-flowered runner bean), but white butter, cannellini or haricot beans would also work.

For British equivalents of the continental meats vital to this dish, see the sources at the back of the book. The chorizo should be a semi-soft cooking chorizo, rather than the eating type, and the blood sausage should be a morcilla or boudin noir sausage in natural skin. These types of blood sausages are less starchy than traditional British black pudding, with a warm, spiced flavour.

Nothing is needed alongside except perhaps a good green salad and a glass of crisp, cold cider or white wine.

Cover the beans with three times their volume of cold water and leave to soak overnight.

When ready to cook, finely chop half the pancetta. Place this in a big, heavy-based casserole pot with the olive oil, onions and garlic and soften over medium heat, until the onions and the pancetta become slightly caramelized – about 20 minutes. Cut the remaining pancetta into chunky 2.5cm cubes.

Drain the beans and add them to the casserole along with the pancetta chunks, herbs and spices. Pour in enough cold water to cover (about 1.5 litres), put the lid on and bring to a rolling boil for 5–10 minutes, then reduce to a bare simmer. Cook gently, partially covered and stirring occasionally, for 1 or 2 hours, until the beans are very nearly soft to their cores (how long this takes will depend on the age and type of beans used).

Add more water every now and then if you need to, so that the beans remain just submerged.

Add the sausages and continue cooking very gently (so they don't burst) for another 30 minutes, until the sausages are fully cooked and the beans are super-creamy yet still holding their shape. Taste a little and season with salt and pepper.

Remove and discard the herbs. Remove the sausages and cut them each into 3 or 4 chunks. Return these to the pot. If the stew seems too liquid, crush some of the beans with a potato masher or fork. Serve in shallow bowls, making sure each person gets at least one chunk of pancetta, chorizo and blood sausage.

Potted Rabbit

MAKES 1 LARGE JAR

1 wild or farmed rabbit,
    jointed into small sections
sea salt and black pepper
500–600ml duck or goose fat
4 large cloves of garlic,
    peeled and sliced
1 small red onion, peeled
    and finely sliced
3 bay leaves
4 sprigs of fresh rosemary
8 sprigs of fresh thyme
2 sprigs of fresh sage
150ml white wine
200–300ml chicken stock
cider vinegar and/or chopped
    capers (optional)

AUGUST TO FEBRUARY IS
BEST FOR WILD RABBIT

Rows and rows of rabbit and hare hang, grey-pelted and wet muzzle down, high above the wide open-fronted, marble-slabbed entrance to my great-uncle's game merchant shop. I am a child but fascinated by the array, holding my mother's hand as she negotiates with my white-aproned uncle over the price of some choice ingredient, only to complain afterwards that he has sold her short.

Rabbit is a supremely tasty, affordable and latterly under-used source of meat protein. It matures quickly without needing much food, so can be an ethical choice. Wild rabbits will be smaller and will take longer to cook. Add the pickled samphire (see page 101) and crusty bread to serve. You could add chopped capers to the mix too.

The recipe is best made the day before and will keep for around a week in the fridge.

Season the clean, dry rabbit with salt and pepper and leave for 30–60 minutes for the flavour to develop.

In a large, heavy casserole, melt 2 tablespoons of the fat and brown the rabbit thoroughly over a medium-high heat, working in batches as space allows. Add the garlic and onion to the pan and arrange all the browned rabbit pieces on top, tucking the herbs between. The amount of liquid and fat you'll need will depend on the size of the rabbit and the pot. Add all the white wine, then the rest of the fat and the stock in turn until the rabbit is completely covered. Bring to a very, very slow simmer (just an occasional bubble breaking the surface) and cook for 2–3 hours, until the rabbit flesh is falling off the bone.

Take the pot off the heat and remove the rabbit pieces. Sieve the stock into a bowl so that the fat rises to the surface. Carefully spoon off the fat for later use. Remove the herbs and spiky bits from the sieve and discard, then mash the onion and garlic to a paste.

Once the rabbit is cool enough to handle, shred the good flesh into very tiny strips in a mixing bowl. Add the onion and garlic mush.

Pour the stock back into the pot and boil to reduce to one quarter of the volume.

Keep tasting – the idea is to reduce to an intensely fragrant liquid to add back and boost the rabbit flavour.

Add a couple of tablespoons of stock to the shredded rabbit, then a couple of tablespoons of still-warm fat. Keep going like this until you have a delicious, coarse paste – you won't need all the quantity. Taste, then season with salt and pepper and cider vinegar or capers to brighten. Look for the balance of flavours you like.

Use any leftover fat for roasting potatoes, delicious surplus stock for soup or stew.

Put the rabbit paste into a large, clean, lidded jar and cover the surface with melted fat. Refrigerate the jar for a few hours, then eat with crunchy toast and some pickles. Use within a week.

GATHER COOK FEAST

Spelt Sourdough with Pumpkin Seeds

MAKES 2 LOAVES

625g, plus 50g warm water

200g sourdough starter,
    well fed, bubbly and raring
    to go (see page 204)

2 tablespoons good-quality
    cold-pressed rapeseed oil

300g wholegrain spelt flour

700g white bread flour (i.e. high-
    protein 'strong' wheat flour)

40g pumpkin seeds

40g sunflower seeds

25g fine sea salt

extra flour for dusting

A delicious sourdough recipe with spelt and pumpkin seeds and enriched with nutty rapeseed oil to try with a newly active starter. I owe much to Anna for this recipe, part of her life generously shared and tutored to me. Now I make this every week and love it. The recipe is based on something similar pioneered by Tartine in San Francisco.

You will need a big, heavy casserole pot of 3.75 litres volume (23cm across x 10cm high) that can tolerate a high oven temperature. For detailed instructions on how to make the required starter and how to fit sourdough beautifully into the rhythm of your life, see pages 201–6.

Weigh 625g of warm water into a large bowl. Carefully add the starter – if it is really active it should float. Stir briefly to combine, then add the oil and flours. Give it a really good mix until no dry patches remain, then cover with a damp cloth and leave for 20 minutes to hydrate.

Now measure in 50g of water, add the seeds and sprinkle over the salt. Use your hand to thoroughly scrunch and mix the dough until everything is evenly distributed.

Cover the bowl again and let the dough rise in a warm place for around 4 hours, until around 50% bigger in volume. Every half an hour turn and fold it like this – reach down, lift up one side, then stretch it up and over the top of the ball of dough to reach the other side, where you can press the end down gently so it stays put. Repeat all the way around the dough, imagining it has four sides. As time progresses the dough should become puffier, lighter, smoother, stronger and easier to handle. Try not to squidge out all the air.

After the dough has risen sufficiently, turn it out on to a lightly floured work surface, divide in two and shape it into two boules by making a series of folds (same method as before and using as little flour as possible) to create a smooth taut surface on the underside.

Heavily flour two large round proving baskets (or a large colander, or a bowl lined with a tea towel). Transfer the boules to the baskets, seam side up. If the seams are gaping, pinch them closed. They should half fill the baskets.

Cover again and let prove in the fridge for 12–16 hours. The boules could rise to more or less fill the baskets. If they haven't quite done that, don't worry – they will rise further in the oven.

Bring the dough out of the fridge. Put your lidded casserole into the oven and heat the oven as hot as it will go. Wait for half an hour for the pot to get really hot. Then carry the smokingly hot pot to somewhere safe. Give the dough a generous sprinkling of flour on top, then carefully tip it into the hot pot with its round smooth side on top. Confidently slash the top a few times using a sharp knife (don't burn yourself). Immediately replace the lid and return the pot to the oven. Reduce the temperature by 10°C or one gas mark and bake for 25 minutes. Then remove the lid, turn the heat down another 10°C or one gas mark and continue baking for a further 20 minutes or so until the crust is a rich brown. Cook one loaf after the other in the same pot.

Cool the loaves completely on a wire rack before cutting. They will easily last a week and will freeze well.

About Sourdough Starters
& Sourdough Bread

Making bread using a sourdough starter is a subtle, complicated, unpredictable process but it's really worth persisting, because the reward of your first sourdough loaf easily makes up for the angst of getting there in the first place. The first batch of starter I made failed to float in the approved manner, but the joy when the second batch floated beautifully – so rewarding!

The process is a three-part one. First make the starter culture. Then use a small quantity of this starter culture to make a leaven, before proceeding to make the sourdough bread proper. In between bread-making batches the culture will keep well in the fridge but you will need to feed it every week or two.

You will need to learn the conditions in your home and where the sourdough culture is likely to be happiest (this was a big problem for me with a cold house), to feed it regularly and learn how it likes to be treated. How your starter behaves will depend on the flour and water you use, the temperature at which you keep it and the frequency at which you feed it. With experience you will learn which conditions are optimum for yours, to create the flavour and texture you want in your bread. Importantly, you need to develop an environment rich with the cultures required for sourdough – the necessary yeasts and bacteria are in the air, in the flour and on the skin, but not in any great quantity until you help them along with your love and tender care. This is important to remember when you have limited success at first – if you try again it will get better and better.

This recipe is for making and keeping the simple wheat starter needed for the recipes for spelt sourdough (see page 199) and malt loaf (see page 207).You can substitute wholemeal spelt or rye flour for wholemeal wheat. If using rye, add a couple of tablespoons more water on days one and two of making your starter. Otherwise the instructions are the same. Wheat starters are often the most active – they will bubble up and then fall down again faster than rye. Rye starters will be slower, but once risen they seem to hold their bubbly strength for slightly longer, both in the starter and in the sourdough bread dough. Spelt starters will be slightly harder to use, because they produce a more sticky dough which is somewhat challenging to knead and manhandle.

A last word: if you'd love to make sourdough but can't get through this first stage, it is easy to buy a sourdough starter – see sources on page 335.

GATHER COOK FEAST

How to Make a Sourdough Starter

It will take about a week to make the starter. During this period it will need feeding with flour and water every day. Many recipes call for fruit (such as raisins or rhubarb) to get the starter going, but they are not necessary. All you need is good flour and water.

There are a few strictures – the better the ingredients, the greater chance you have of succeeding first time. The bacteria and yeasts required for a sourdough culture do not thrive in competition with chemicals. For success, use only filtered or still spring water and organic flour (stone-ground if possible), which will have all original nutrients and bacteria intact and will be free of those unwanted chemicals. An ambient temperature of 18–22°C is important for the yeasts to flourish and develop. If your rooms are colder than this, find a warmer place to keep the culture while it is growing. Airing cupboards, over a radiator or on the fridge where warm air emerges are all possible places – to be sure, use a thermometer.

For accuracy, weigh the water, rather than using a measuring jug.

Sourdough lore also suggests the stirring implement should be wood or plastic rather than metal, which may inhibit the culture.

You'll need a good container big enough to hold around 1 litre of liquid, with a lid. Plastic is best to avoid breakage and subsequent loss of beautiful culture.

Day 1

75g cool (not freezing) water
50g wholewheat flour

Measure the water and flour into the tub and mix well with a small rubber spatula or wooden spoon. Cover loosely with the lid and leave out in your warm place.

Days 2–6

Each day, add 50ml of cool (not freezing) water and 50g of wholewheat flour to the pot and stir well. Cover loosely with the lid and leave out at room temperature.

When making a starter for the first time, sometimes the culture stalls after a day or two of initial activity and a slick of brown liquid may develop on the surface. If this happens, pour off all the mixture except 1 tablespoon (don't skimp here, the culture will grow from this 1 tablespoon and the high proportion of new nutrient to culture is vital to get the starter going again). Then start the feeding regime from day 1 until it is healthy and active. Stirring it well and leaving the culture open to the air or in warm sunshine for an hour or two (to catch any passing yeasts) can also help it develop well. You can use this method at any time if the starter looks unhappy.

By day 6 or 7 your starter should be very active – full of bubbles, smelling pleasantly sour and rising to nearly three times its volume. If so, it is ready to use for making the first sourdough bread. If you want to make bread immediately, go straight to making a leaven. Alternatively, feed the starter and keep it in the fridge until you have enough time to make the sourdough. If it never develops bubbles this means something is inhibiting the fermentation, such as chemicals in the water, overly refined flour or too cold a room. In that case it's best to try again with a new batch. It's worth persisting.

Keeping a Starter

In between bread-making sessions the starter culture will keep well in the fridge, but it will need feeding every week or two to keep it alive and happy. The feeding routine is the same as for creating the leaven. Just follow the instructions below, then return it to the fridge with the lid loosely on the pot. If you leave the starter in the fridge for more than 2 weeks it may stop bubbling and develop that slick of water on the top. It may still revive by adding a feed (as below) to 1 tablespoon of the original culture.

To Make a Leaven

To use your starter to raise a loaf of bread in place of commercial yeast, it needs to be really active. You can't use your starter straight from the fridge or when it is desperate for its next feed. It needs to be at the peak of its activity and bubbling up to at least twice its volume. In this state it is called a leaven.

200g cool (not freezing) water
100g strong white bread flour
100g wholewheat flour

Scrape out all except a heaped tablespoon of the starter (around 50g). The discarded starter could be given to a friend so they can start their own, or used to make sourdough pancakes, but it won't be active enough to raise a loaf of bread so you may end up simply throwing it away.

Place the tub on scales and measure in the water. Give it a good stir to dissolve the starter and clean down the sides of the tub. Now measure in the flours and stir them in really well so no dry patches remain. Scrape down the sides of the pot and close loosely with the lid.

Leave the tub out at room temperature (18–22°C) until it is really bubbly, risen to at least twice its volume and smelling pleasantly sour. How long this takes will depend on your starter and your room temperature. It will probably take

7–9 hours – all day when you are at work – and, hopefully, be ready to make the dough when you return in the evening.

To test it is ready to use, very carefully lift out a dollop of starter and gently place it in a bowl of water. If it floats, the leaven is ready to use in your bread recipe. If it sinks, the leaven may need more time, or it may have been left too long, in which case you should start the refreshing process again. If you are desperate to make your very first batch of bread, there is no shame in supplementing a teaspoon of commercial yeast as an insurance policy. The sourdough starter may take a few batches before developing the maturity to raise bread brilliantly every time.

If you want to continue your starter afterwards, don't use it all up in the bread recipe. Save the last tablespoon in the pot, feed it (see page 205) and store it as usual.

Tips for Making Sourdough & How to Fit It Around a Busy Life

First thing in the morning: feed the starter and leave it out to rise. *Early evening*: make the dough. *Last thing before bed*: shape the dough and leave to prove in the fridge overnight. *The next morning, any time*: bake.

The dough is very quick to assemble if you have electronic scales. Weigh everything into the bowl one by one; tare the scales to 0g each time.

Shaping is the only hard part. The dough is quite soft, so it takes a little getting used to. To make it easier, follow these tips. Shape with clean, dry hands – if they get sticky, stop and clean them before proceeding. Use as little flour as possible; if you incorporate too much the bread will become dense, and the folds won't stick and hold in place. Be reasonably gentle with the dough but act quickly and confidently; if you stay with your hands on the dough for more than a couple of seconds they will stick to it. Use a dough scraper to help move the dough, and to clean the table afterwards.

If you want to be serious about making bread it is good to use a basket for proving the dough. These are traditionally wicker or bamboo. But any basket lined with a good cloth would work. I have a special linen cloth in my proving basket that never gets washed, adding to the culture-rich environment. If your house is cold, find a good warm place to start off the first rise or warm the flour first.

Cooking a round sourdough loaf in a pot vastly improves the rise, shape and crust of the loaf.

Sourdough Malt Loaf

MAKES 3 LOAVES

360g warm water

4 large eggs

140g treacle

140g malt extract

50g soft brown sugar

100g melted butter, plus extra
for greasing the tins

24g fine salt

140g raisins

200g sourdough starter,
well fed, bubbly and raring
to go (see page 204)

200g barley flour

800g white bread flour (i.e. high-
protein 'strong' wheat flour)

This is a recreation of the intensely malty Soreen malt loaf of childhood teatime memories but using a sourdough starter to provide a more complex flavour and a moist crumb.

Malt is extracted as sticky, thick syrup from sprouting barley: rich sugars released by the germination process.

As usual for sourdough, the ambient temperature is important for development of the dough. You'll need a place that hovers between 18°C and 22°C – if this isn't your home, perhaps an airing cupboard or over a radiator will serve. Malt loaf freezes brilliantly, well wrapped.

Combine the water, eggs, treacle, malt, sugar, butter and salt in a medium-large bowl and whisk well to combine. Stir in the raisins and starter, then the flours, and mix well until no dry patches remain.

Cover with a plastic bag or damp tea towel and leave for 20 minutes, to allow the flours to fully hydrate. Grease three loaf tins (22 x 12 x 6cm) with butter.

Knead the dough briefly to get the gluten development started. You can do this on the table with the help of a dough scraper, as it will be very sticky. Or keep it in the bowl and use your hand or a large flexible spatula to repeatedly lift up the edge of the dough and fold it over the top. Either way the key thing is simply to stretch and fold the dough a few times. It should begin to feel less shaggy and somewhat smoother and stronger.

Divide the dough between the tins and use a wet hand to gently pat it into shape. The dough should half fill the tins. Cover with a plastic bag or damp tea towel and leave in a warm place to rise. This will take 8–12 hours, depending on the strength of your starter and the ambient temperature, so can be done overnight. The dough should rise to not quite fill the tins.

Heat the oven to 190°C/170°C fan/gas 5. Bake the breads for around 1 hour, until well risen, deep brown and cooked through. You can test by inserting a digital probe thermometer into the centre: it should read at least 95°C. Tip the loaves out of their tins and cool on a wire rack. Eat toasted or untoasted, but always with a layer of good butter on top.

Ginger & Pumpkin Seed Shortbread

MAKES 12 FINGERS

120g wholemeal spelt flour,
    plus extra for rolling
45g fine cornmeal
60g golden caster sugar
125g butter, chopped into small cubes
1½ teaspoons ground ginger
a pinch of sea salt
25g pumpkin seeds, toasted
    in a dry pan until just golden

Crisp, with a satisfying crunch and textured a little like a digestive biscuit, this shortbread is gingery and buttery, with crispy pumpkin seeds hidden in each slice. It is easy and quick to make – the only difficulty may be waiting for the shortbread to cool before eating. The spelt flour and fine cornmeal add bite.

These are even better the next day. Shortbread biscuits are lovely with all manner of puddings; or eat them on their own.

Heat the oven to 190°C/170°C fan/gas 5.

Put all the ingredients except the pumpkin seeds into a large bowl. Rub the butter into the dry ingredients, as if you are making pastry. After a short while the mixture will begin to resemble breadcrumbs and all the lumps of butter will be incorporated. Now add the toasted pumpkin seeds. Press all the lumps together until you end up with a ball of dough. Collect any little crumbs and squeeze them into the ball.

Cut a piece of baking paper large enough for the baking tray you plan to use. Put a little flour on the rolling pin and roll out the shortbread on the baking paper to make a square approximately 20 x 20cm and around 8mm thick. As you roll you will find the edges cracking and breaking – stabilize and straighten up the edges with your fingers as you go.

When you have finished, gently lift the paper loaded with the rolled shortbread on to a baking tray and use a kitchen knife to mark out 12 biscuit shapes, cutting through to the base of the shortbread.

Cook in the oven for 15–20 minutes, until cooked through and golden.

The lines you have drawn will have become blurred during the cooking, so re-cut the shapes of the biscuits, then leave the baking tray out for them to cool.

Hedgerow Pudding

SERVES 4–5

400g blackberries
200g raspberries
100g damsons or plums
75g hazelnuts or cobnuts
    (pre-shelled weight), shelled,
    toasted, skinned, chopped
150g sugar
8 slices of slightly stale white
    bread, crusts removed
single cream, to serve

AUGUST TO SEPTEMBER
FOR BLACKBERRIES, LATE
AUGUST TO SEPTEMBER
FOR DAMSONS

My favourite version of summer pudding is made with blackberries in the autumn, but then it can't be called summer. This is my version with mixed wild soft fruits and nuts, which I am renaming in honour of the humble hedgerow.

Blackberrying is the sort of foraging everyone knows and loves. Raspberries, damsons and plums can be found in the wild too, if you are lucky. The damsons add a wonderful extra sharpness to the fruit but can be hard to find. In need, replace with a good sharp plum.

For a full foraged hedgerow experience, wet and pale hazelnuts or Kent cobnuts can be a delicious, delicate choice, or use regular shop-bought hazelnuts for a more toasty taste.

Slightly stale bread is helpful to hold the pudding together and avoid gumminess, but you can leave out a few slices to dry out in advance of making this, or keep a sliced loaf in the freezer.

Make the day before, or at least 6 hours before you plan to eat it.

Prepare the fruit. If the blackberries or raspberries are foraged ones, pick over them carefully and remove any overripe or sharp prickly ones and any stowaway bugs. Remove the stones from the damsons by cutting the flesh away from the stone.

Put the fruit, nuts and sugar into a heavy lidded pan and cook over a low heat, until the fruit has given off its liquid and the sugar has dissolved. Turn the heat up a touch and cook for a further 3–5 minutes, until the damsons are tender. Taste the mixture and add a little sugar if needed (keep it fruity).

Line a 750ml basin with clingfilm, with enough hanging over the edges to fold over the top and twist together. Then line the basin all the way around with the white bread, keeping one slice for the top.

Strain the fruit mixture, retaining the juice. Pour a little of the juice all around the inside of the bread slices in the basin, to make the bread as purple as possible with the juice. Don't worry if there are some white bits left on the outside, you will have some leftover juice to deal with those later. Then put all the strained solids into the hollow. Pop the last slice of bread over the top and fold in all the other bits of bread. Pull

up the edges of clingfilm and twist them tightly together. Find a saucer small enough to fit inside the basin, then put a heavy object on top of the saucer and refrigerate overnight.

When ready to eat, open out the clingfilm, put a plate on top and invert to turn out, gently pulling the pudding out using the edges of the clingfilm.

Pour a little of the remaining juice over the pudding to cover any random white areas and serve the rest with each portion.

Serve with single cream.

Two Malted
Ice Creams

EACH RECIPE SERVES 4

For malted brown bread ice cream
100g brown bread,
    having removed crusts
25g butter
35g light brown sugar
150ml Jersey or Guernsey
    full cream milk
180ml double cream
50g caster sugar
2 egg yolks
2 large tablespoons barley
    malt extract
lemon zest (optional)

For simple malt ice cream
200ml Jersey or Guernsey
    full cream milk
50g caster sugar
100g sweetened condensed milk
3 tablespoons barley malt extract
250ml double cream

The idea of a malt ice cream had been living in my mind for some time, and I worked on version after version in search of the taste I had imagined. Here are my two favourites – a simple one, and a richer one with toasted brown breadcrumbs, both resonant of the warmth of the malting floor and our beery heritage. Condensed milk is thick and sticky with added sugar and is distinctly different from evaporated milk, which has no added sugar.

For instructions on how to make ice cream by hand, see page 112.

Malted Brown Bread Ice Cream

Put the brown bread into a food processor and whizz to medium crumbs.

Melt the butter and the light brown sugar in a smallish frying pan, over a medium heat, until just darkening and melted together. Take the pan off the heat and add the breadcrumbs, stirring all around to ensure the crumbs are fully coated with the butter and sugar mixture. Then put the pan back on the heat and continue to toast for around 12–15 minutes, until golden and crisp. Leave to cool.

Next make the custard. Whisk up the milk, cream, caster sugar and egg yolks in a pan over a low to medium heat. Stir constantly and efficiently until the custard coats the back of a spoon. Take the custard off the heat and stir in the malt extract. Leave to cool.

Once everything is cool, mix together and churn in an ice cream maker until done. As a variation, some lemon zest is a possible addition.

Simple Malt Ice Cream

Heat the milk and sugar in a small pan until the sugar is melted. Take off the heat and mix in the condensed milk, malt extract and cream. Leave to cool, then churn in an ice cream maker or make by hand (see page 112).

Curate's Pudding

SERVES 6

60g butter, at room temperature,
    plus a little extra for greasing
120g granulated sugar
6 tablespoons cold mashed potato
2 eggs, beaten
zest and juice of 1 lemon
a pinch of sea salt
2 tablespoons milk

This pudding comes from an age when re-use of leftovers was sacrosanct. We are familiar with puddings that use up leftover bread; here is a somewhat unlikely pudding created to use up mashed potato. I found this while browsing a very battered, handed-down copy of Mrs Beeton, although, as most of her recipes were purloined from elsewhere, it no doubt had an earlier origin.

I can't imagine boiling potatoes especially to make this, but it is a simple, sizzling, gorgeous pudding, which is very easy to make with leftover mash. I have no idea why it is called curate's pudding. I imagine a single, black-garbed fellow abstemiously spooning this pudding, attended by a sober, aproned cook. But that's just me.

Heat the oven to 200°C/180°C fan/gas 6 and grease a 20cm pie dish with a little of the butter.

Cream the butter and sugar with an electric whisk in a bowl until you have a thick and grainy mixture. Stir in the mashed potato, then add the beaten eggs bit by bit until all is incorporated.

Finally add the lemon zest and juice, the pinch of salt and the milk.

Pour the mixture into the pie dish and cook in the oven for 30–35 minutes, until golden around the edges, gently firm and sizzling.

Eat just warm, with a little thin cream and maybe a few autumn berries on the side.

Bramble & Bay
Jelly Pots

MAKES 4 POTS

500g blackberries
100g sugar
5 fresh bay leaves
2 tablespoons water
10g gelatine leaves

AUGUST TO SEPTEMBER
FOR BLACKBERRIES

Foraged blackberries sometimes need a little bolstering in a poor, cloudy year, when they can often fail to develop acidity and sweetness. Blackberries are now easily foraged from the supermarket as well – some good juicy varieties are available in the autumn months.

Here blackberries are combined with bay leaves, the fruity sweetness contrasting well with the sanctified, slightly medicinal bay taste, in a recipe for juicy, jellied pots, stuffed with fruit. The best pots to use are roundish individual anodized pudding moulds, because the conductivity of the metal allows them to give up their cargo easily. But ramekins or even a teacup would work too. It's hard to weigh gelatine leaves accurately because they are individually so light. The solution is to weigh the whole packet and divide by the number of leaves to calculate the weight of each leaf.

Put the blackberries, sugar, bay leaves and water into a pan and cook gently, covered, over a medium heat until the sugar has dissolved and the blackberries are tender. Check the sweetness and adjust to taste (different blackberries may vary in levels of sweetness).

Take off the heat and leave the bay leaves to steep for a few hours.

Remove the bay leaves. Soak the leaves of gelatine in cold water for 10 minutes until soft. While they soak, warm the blackberry mixture again without boiling hard.

Squeeze the water out of the gelatine leaves and then stir them into the hot blackberry mixture quickly (don't continue to stir once incorporated, because it may cause the gelatine to become stringy). Lift some of the liquid in a spoon to check that the gelatine is all melted. Pour into small pots and refrigerate for a few hours or overnight.

To turn out, put the pots into a shallow dish of hot water to slightly soften the edges. Run a knife around the edge and invert them on to individual plates.

Eat with a thin cream, and perhaps the Lenten almond biscuits on page 64.

MOSS UNDERSTOREY
CHESTNUT DAMSON
FELLED MUSHROOM
LITTERFALL SMOKE
HEATH & WOOD FERN

PORK UMBER BARK
COBNUT CRAB APPLE
CANOPY DIM LIGHT
LATE BERRY PLUM
BRANCHED PIGEON

The pre-Neolithic landscape of Britain was entirely clothed in woodland. Beech, birch, oak, lime and hazel swelled over hills and pooled in valleys. The wild wood was thick, with settlement only on the high ground. The forest was a treacherous, difficult place. What evidence there is suggests food sources were rich and varied – leaves and roots of wild plants, berries, nuts and game. Later, man used fire and axe to clear trees in order to sow. Smoke rose as the forest receded. Now Britain has less woodland than the average in Europe (happily the percentage is expanding). We may have destroyed most of our woodland, but we still feel passionately about our woods: as evidenced in the myths of Sherwood and the recent rebellion against a forest sell-off by the government. If man no longer tilled the land, forest would resume within a lifetime. It's a place of ancient seclusion.

The foods of the forest and woodland are among my favourites: chestnuts and walnuts; elderberries and damsons; rowanberries; apples; wild boar and forest-raised pork; and, of course, mushrooms – wild and cultivated.

Pigs love the cover of woods, the shade protecting their sensitive backs from sun. Pork easily takes the taste of the animal's diet too – from apples or acorns scattered on the forest floor. Why would we choose industrially farmed pigs whose bleak life – raised on grills, fed concentrate and unable to truffle and dig – serves only profit and mass production? This type of farming brings lowest-cost pork to the shelves but at great cost to the animal and the quality of the meat. Rather eat less and better and source pork from pigs allowed to roam. Such pork is often from heritage breeds such as Berkshire, Gloucester Old Spot and Large Black, each of which has its own character and flavour to explore.

The smell of wood smoke directly feeds an atavistic need for cooking with fire. In the thick oak woods that surrounded the cottage where I started my married life, there were abandoned platforms, the vestiges of a local logging and charcoal-burning industry. The woods will have been full of fragrant smoke. This is the chapter where you'll find instructions for hot-smoking, as well as three recipes to try: first hot-smoking bacon; then pigeon for a salad, with pear, endive and chestnuts; and finally potatoes to accompany bay-wrapped pork. Smoking is an easy, rewarding way to add layers of subtle flavour to food – and to recreate the feeling of an autumn wood in your kitchen. I hope you give it a try.

Autumn Minestrone

SERVES 6

250g dried red haricot beans
  (or red kidney or borlotti)
2 tablespoons olive oil
2 onions, peeled and finely chopped
2 carrots, peeled and finely chopped
3 sticks of celery, finely chopped
4 cloves of garlic, peeled
  and very finely chopped
2 bay leaves, fresh if possible
3–5 sprigs of fresh thyme and/or
  winter or summer savory
2 medium to large potatoes
  (around 300g), peeled and
  finely chopped
300g smoked pork ribs
½ x 400g tin of chopped tomatoes
sea salt and black pepper
peppery extra virgin olive oil
elderberry vinegar (see page 259),
  or aged balsamic vinegar
roughly chopped fresh parsley leaves

This soup needs long and slow cooking – and it is much better reheated, so make ahead of time.

The red haricot bean (actually a deep garnet colour) is British grown, smaller and more delicate than the better-known red kidney or borlotti beans. I favour the red haricot for those reasons, but all three will perform, breaking down into creamy richness during the long cook. The method specifies dried, but if using tinned (2 x 400g tins), skip the soaking and boiling. Note that dried red beans should always be boiled hard for 10 minutes to neutralize traces of toxins present in the skins of some dried beans.

Smoked pork ribs can be easily homemade using the method on page 232, or ordered from a specialist butcher. They make all the difference to this dish. For a vegetarian version, replace the pork ribs with several saved umami-rich old Parmesan rinds (but remove before eating).

Soak the beans in three times their volume of cold water for 8–12 hours.

Heat the oil in a heavy-bottomed casserole pot. Add the onions, carrots and celery and soften over a medium heat for 10–15 minutes. Add the garlic and herbs and cook for another 5 minutes, stirring to prevent sticking.

Drain the beans and add them to the pot along with 1 litre of fresh water. Increase the heat and let the beans boil vigorously for 10 minutes. Reduce the heat, then cover and leave to simmer gently until the beans are just tender but still holding their shape, around 40 minutes.

Stir in the potatoes, ribs and tomatoes, put the lid back on and continue simmering for at least another hour (preferably two), until the beans and potatoes are starting to fall apart and the meat on the ribs is tender. Remove the bay leaves, herb stalks and ribs. Use a couple of forks to shred the meat off the bones. Return the shredded meat to the pot and add some water if the soup is too thick. Stir well to encourage the beans and potatoes to fall apart. Taste and season with salt and pepper.

Ladle a serving into each bowl and pour over a little peppery extra virgin olive oil and elderberry vinegar. Sprinkle with parsley.

Dark Stouty Mushroom Soup

SERVES 4 AS A SMALL BOWL,
2–3 HUNGRY PEOPLE FOR SUPPER

The stock
750ml water
20g dried porcini
1 carrot, peeled and chopped
1 stick of celery, chopped
1 red onion, peeled and chopped
a small bunch of fresh parsley
2 fresh sage leaves
2 bay leaves
2 sprigs of fresh thyme
12 peppercorns
2 cloves of garlic,
   peeled and left whole

The soup
40g salted butter
250g portobello or chestnut
   mushrooms, sliced
1 onion, peeled and chopped
4 small tomatoes, chopped
sea salt and black pepper
1 tablespoon plain flour
1 bay leaf
300ml mushroom stock (see above)
   (or vegetable or chicken stock)
1 tablespoon tomato purée
250ml sweet, dark stout
3 tablespoons roughly
   chopped fresh parsley
a few spoonfuls of crème fraîche
   and/or grated Parmesan, to finish

This is a rich, dark and appropriately autumnal soup. The choice of stout is important – choose one which is not too bitter, but rather sweet and dark.

If you have time, homemade mushroom stock will add complexity, but the soup is still very good with a vegetable or chicken stock. The mushroom stock can be made in quantity and frozen for later use. Use it for an earthy fungi risotto or stew, or to add another layer of flavour to the wild rice and mushroom salad on page 236, or the dark lentil soup on page 278.

The stock
Put everything into a sturdy, lidded pan, bring to the boil, then cover and simmer gently for 1 hour. Cool and strain through a kitchen paperlined sieve. Squeeze out the vegetables to express all the stock.

Save 300ml of stock for the soup. Freeze the rest for other meals.

The soup
Melt the butter over a medium heat in a heavy pan and brown the mushrooms, turning them often, until soft and golden. Then add the onion and cook for 5–10 minutes more, until translucent. Finally add the tomatoes and cook for another 5–10 minutes, until they are soft and fragrant. Season a little with salt and black pepper.

Stir in the flour and cook gently for 2 minutes, then add the bay leaf, stock, tomato purée and stout. Give everything a good stir as you bring the soup back to a simmer. Continue to cook together for 10–15 minutes.

Taste the soup again to check the seasoning and adjust as needed. If the stout has left the soup a little bitter, add a small knob of butter to soften the flavour.

Toss in most of the chopped parsley, allow it to soften, then ladle into bowls. Top with a spoonful of crème fraîche and a little more chopped parsley. Some finely grated Parmesan on the top is also delicious. Serve hot, with chunks of crusty, buttered bread.

A Little Wood Smoke in Your Kitchen —
The Art of Hot-Smoking at Home

Until I began writing this book I had never hot-smoked, but now I'm thoroughly smitten. The whole process is easy and utterly winning. Gorgeous woodsy, smoky flavours scent the kitchen: the meat, fish or vegetables are infused with subtle tastes and slowly cooked at the same time. The quantity of smoke produced by the smouldering wood powder is minimal – there is no need for an extractor fan, but you might like to open your windows if you have a sensitive smoke alarm.

It is important to know the difference between hot and cold smoking. Cold-smoking involves keeping the food in a cold smoky atmosphere for a prolonged period of time. It doesn't cook the food at all. This method of smoking is more complicated and isn't covered in this book.

Hot-smoking involves first curing meat or fish (vegetables don't need a cure) in a light mix of salt and sometimes sugar, then cooking them gently in warm smoke until done. The cure draws some of the moisture from the flesh, enabling the smoke to penetrate, and improves the texture of the meat or fish. Once cooked, eat the hot-smoked food within a day or so – this is not a preserving method.

Equipment

Hot-smoking can be achieved with relatively simple equipment – which can be bought or cobbled together out of what you have. You'll need a two-layered vessel to smoke in, some wood dust to provide the smoked flavour and heat from a hob or gas ring. Special stovetop smokers and wood dust are available from the suppliers listed on page 336.

You can improvise by finding an old or cheap double steamer saucepan – the sort with holes in the top pan. Or use a colander over a normal saucepan. Or any old pan with a grill cut to fit, leaving a 3–5cm gap underneath for the smoking wood dust.

Ideally the top level should have some holes for the smoke to permeate upwards and a surface that can be oiled. So if your Heath Robinson DIY has involved a grill for the top layer, you may need to cover this with a sheet of foil into which you pierce some holes.

In each case the top level holds the food, and the bottom level takes the wood dust on a sheet of foil. Foil is useful to prevent staining of the pan and also to lift out the wood dust once spent. Then the whole thing sits on your stovetop for a heat source or over a fire or barbecue outside in the summer.

Wood Dust

It is important to use special food grade wood dust for hot-smoking. This will be untreated and suitable for hot-smoking. Some woods contain toxins that make them unsuitable for smoking (willow and most soft woods). So buy from a reputable supplier.

There are a large variety of woods to choose from, each imparting its own flavour. Woods are available in shavings, chips and in dust form – choose dust form for a simple and easy release of smoke without pre-soaking.

Here are a few favourites:
Apple Wood – complex, sweet, fruity and dense
Oak – the most familiar fragrance, versatile and good with meats
Alder – delicate, sweetish fragrance, perfect with fish and poultry

How to Hot-Smoke

Meat and fish may sometimes be lightly cured first, using a cure from one of the recipes, or just dusted with salt and left for 10–50 minutes depending on size. Vegetables may be hot-smoked from raw, or first cooked, oiled and then smoked (see smoked potatoes, page 246).

Warm the smoker on a low heat until wisps of smoke appear. Rinse off the cure from the meat or fish, pat dry, then lower on to the oiled surface of the top pan. Cover with a lid to trap the smoke in the top section. Keep the heat low, just enough to keep the dust gently smouldering. If the heat gets too high you'll have acrid flavours in the food. Stop smoking as soon as the wood dust is spent and completely black, or it will taint the food with bitterness. If needed, replace with fresh dust to continue.

Continue to cook as specified in the individual recipes. Try hot-smoked trout (see page 36), hot-smoked pigeon breasts (see page 231), hot-smoked potatoes (see page 246) and hot-smoked bacon or ribs (see page 232).

Chestnut Pancakes

MAKES 10–12 PANCAKES

200g chestnut flour
1½ teaspoons baking powder
a pinch of sea salt
1 egg
2 tablespoons maple syrup
225ml milk
hazelnut oil

The need for a one-pan breakfast brought these tender, nutty and flavoursome pancakes into the world. Chestnuts are less fatty than other nuts, with a remarkably high level of vitamin C. Expect the finished pancake to have a textured, grainy finish, as chestnuts don't have gluten like wheat flour.

Maple syrup and hazelnut oil add to the woodsy flavour. Try to find the best proper maple syrup you can, because it does make a difference. Real maple syrup is tapped from trees and the watery sap reduced to a fraction of its original volume. Helpfully, Canada and the US have now standardized their grading system, which is first by level and then by colour. If you love a nerdy exploration there are further distinctions based on farm, first tap or second and so on.

Put the dry ingredients into a basin and make a well in the centre. Break the egg into the centre of the well and add the maple syrup. Mix thoroughly while gradually adding the milk, until you've made a smooth batter and all the milk is used up. The consistency should be like extra thick cream. Leave the mixture to stand for 15 minutes or so for the flour to swell and soften.

Heat a heavy-bottomed pan or skillet. Brush hazelnut oil on the hot surface of the pan and leave for a moment to warm through. Then, using a small ladle or cup, pour the batter into the pan to make 5–6cm pancakes. Pour in as many as will fit, but leaving enough free space to turn them without smearing.

Continue to cook over a medium heat until bubbles appear on the surface of the pancakes and the underside is golden brown. Use a metal slice or spatula to loosen, then turn them over with a quick flip and cook on the other side.

When cooked, lift them out of the pan and tuck them into a clean folded tea towel to keep warm while you cook the rest of the pancakes.

Eat these simply with softened sea-salted butter. But the addition of jam, marmalade or honey is delicious too. Or combine with a dribble of maple syrup, berries and crisp bacon.

Pigeon, Pear, Chestnut & Radicchio Salad

SERVES 4–6

The smoked pigeon breasts
8 juniper berries
¼ teaspoon black peppercorns
¼ teaspoon coriander seeds
1 teaspoon sugar
2 teaspoons sea salt
1 small dried bay leaf, torn
    into several pieces
2 teaspoons maple syrup
4 wild pigeon breasts
    (total weight around 250g)
3 tablespoons apple wood
    sawdust, for smoking

The salad
2 large, perfectly ripe pears
a knob of butter
2 tablespoons maple syrup
200g cooked chestnuts, each
    broken into 2 or 3 pieces
flaky sea salt
2–3 small heads or 1 big one
    of radicchio di Treviso,
    leaves separated and washed
2 heads of white Belgian endive,
    leaves separated and washed
2 handfuls of watercress (around 80g),
    washed and large stems removed

The dressing
2 tablespoons lemon juice
1 tablespoon balsamic or
    elderberry vinegar (see page 259)
2 tablespoons maple syrup
4 tablespoons extra virgin olive oil
2 rounded teaspoons grainy mustard
salt and black pepper, to taste

I love this: the sweet, sour, bitter and smoky flavours of this salad go so well together, as do the russet, amber and pale green colours. Serve it in a big bowl or platter in the centre of the table to share.

In August and September our elder trees, loaded with shiny deep black berries, attract a stream of fat pigeons to gorge on the fruit. We have never dared to cull one (soft-hearted), but imagine the elderberry-infused flesh to be at its most succulent just then. Wild pigeon are game, but regarded as a pest (from their behaviour on the elderberry bush, you can see why) so there is no close season. It is also lovely without the pigeon.

Grind together the juniper, peppercorns, coriander, sugar, salt and bay in a mortar to make a coarse powder. Stir in the maple syrup to make a paste, then daub this all over the pigeon breasts and leave at room temperature to cure for 30–40 minutes (no longer – they will firm up). Carefully brush the cure off the meat with kitchen paper.

Follow the instructions for hot-smoking the pigeon breasts given on page 227. Using apple wood dust, hot-smoke over a very low heat for 10 minutes. Flip the breasts over and cook for another 10 minutes. This should give you medium to medium-rare breasts, depending on their thickness. Remove the meat and let it cool for a few minutes, then slice thinly on an angle, against the grain of the meat.

Make the dressing by whisking together all the ingredients in a small jug. Quarter, core and slice the pears and toss them with around half the dressing in a small bowl. Leave to absorb the flavours for a few minutes.

Heat the butter and maple syrup in a small frying pan over a medium-high heat. Add the chestnuts and cook for 5 minutes, tossing occasionally. Finish with a generous sprinkle of flaky salt. Cut or tear any particularly large radicchio or endive leaves into two or three pieces, then gently toss all the leaves with the remaining dressing. Taste a leaf and add more salt, pepper, oil or vinegar if needed. Finally build up the salad on a big platter in multiple layers of leaves, pears, pigeon and chestnuts, pouring over any remaining dressing from the pear bowl if you like.

Curing & Smoking Your Own
Streaky Bacon or Pork Belly Ribs

Last Christmas, while hosting a houseful of people, no fewer than three guests brought with them home-cured bacon to share. And they were all delicious. And they were all different. Having worked on the fringes of fashion in my career I am repeatedly amazed by how trends and movements start, swell, flourish and fade over time. Is humanity like a flock of starlings, communicating to each other wordlessly, but nevertheless moving in a twisting, surging, but more or less directed way? Every morning we had a tasting of each successive batch, enjoying this portion of soft, fresh back bacon; those rashers of smoked or air-dried streaky. It's obviously the moment for bacon curing.

To make your own streaky bacon you will need a nice piece of pork belly. The pork belly ribs needed for the autumn minestrone on page 223 are cured and smoked in the same way. In each case weigh the meat and use the appropriate proportion of the cure below.

You can become an expert very quickly and later add different flavours to the basic cure – thyme, garlic, cloves and fennel seeds are all good additions.

Cure for 1kg of pork
2 rounded teaspoons black peppercorns
2 rounded teaspoons juniper berries
2 dried bay leaves, torn into pieces
½ a nutmeg, finely grated
200g fine sea salt
200g brown sugar

Grind the peppercorns, juniper and bay leaves to a coarse powder with a mortar and pestle. Mix in the nutmeg, salt and sugar.

Rub the cure mix all over the meat and place it in a plastic food bag. Add any remaining cure and seal. Put the bag inside a dish (because it will leak) and stash away in the bottom of the fridge – for 4 days for a thin piece of pork belly or 5 days for a thick piece of pork belly (ask your butcher if you're not sure what's thick or thin). Every day, rub the bag and turn it over so as to massage the cure mix into the meat. It will give off a lot of water. After the required time, remove the pork from the bag and rinse in cold water to flush off most of the cure mix. Pat dry with kitchen paper, then leave unwrapped in the fridge overnight to dry off. See opposite for storage of cured bacon.

Or add more complexity by air-drying or smoking. These are either/or options and not designed to be combined.

To Air-Dry

Find a protected cold airy space. Winter is the best time to air-dry, as the outdoor temperature must remain reliably under 16°C. An outdoor shed, garage or similar would work. If you are keen, make a curing box to hang outside in the breeze. Construct it like an old-fashioned meat safe – a timber frame covered with wire mesh with a lockable door and a roof to exclude dextrous rats and keep the contents dry.

Hang the bacon up using a butcher's hook, wire or string threaded through a hole made in one corner. If you plan to hang it in an open space, make a bag out of muslin or cheesecloth to drape around the bacon to guard it from insects (large enough so the bacon doesn't touch the edges).

Leave to air-dry for a week or two. The bacon will lose weight as moisture is lost to the air (the rate at which this happens will depend on the humidity of the air), the flavours will concentrate and the flesh will become firmer. Give it the occasional squeeze to judge how firm it's becoming. If white mould starts to appear, wipe it off with kitchen paper soaked in vinegar. If mould of any other colour appears, or the bacon develops an unpleasant smell, throw it away. Don't leave the bacon too long or it will become overly salty and hard.

To Hot-Smoke

See the guidance notes for hot-smoking on page 227. You will probably need to cut the belly into pieces to fit inside your hot-smoker. Smoke in batches for 30–40 minutes each, until the piece of bacon takes on a lovely golden tinge. Stop smoking when most of the wood dust has turned black, to avoid acrid flavours infusing into the meat. Store as below.

To Store Bacon

Fresh, air-dried or smoked bacon should be wrapped in clingfilm or grease-proof paper, kept in the fridge, then sliced into rashers or cut into lardons as needed. It will last at least 10 days. If white mould starts to appear, wipe it off with kitchen paper soaked in vinegar and use up the bacon promptly. If mould of any other colour appears, or the bacon develops an unpleasant smell, throw it away.

Roasted Radicchio with Goat's Cheese, Black Figs & Cobnuts

SERVES 4 AS A LIGHT MEAL
OR AS A STARTER

2 medium heads of Chioggia
    radicchio, coarse
    outer leaves removed
6 large figs, hard stalks removed
150g log of goat's cheese,
    cut into 4 equal rounds
120g Kent cobnuts, shelled
    (yielding 40g nuts)

The dressing
1 tablespoon good, thick
    balsamic vinegar
2 tablespoons olive oil
1 clove of garlic, peeled,
    finely chopped and mashed
    a little with some sea salt
    using the back of a knife
sea salt and black pepper

SEPTEMBER TO OCTOBER
FOR KENT COBNUTS

The magical seasonal conjunction of glossy deep red boules of bitter Chioggia radicchio, soft sweet Turkish figs and moist Kent cobnuts is an invitation to combine these three wonderful flavours. Sweet goat's cheese and figs beautifully offset the bitterness of the radicchio, roasted together until soft and melting.

Kent cobnuts can be found in supermarkets for a very short time in the autumn. Their soft pistachio colours are beautiful. Once shelled, the soft, tender nuts can be lightly toasted. If you can't find cobnuts, regular toasted hazelnuts will work well too.

The quality of the goat's cheese is important: very fresh or super-dry, hard older goat's cheese won't melt in the right way. Look for a well-made cheese with a good taste, a yielding density and a good, bloomed rind. Stawley, Dorstone and Innes are recommended – all made by devoted enthusiasts from unpasteurized milk.

Heat the oven to 200°C/180°C fan/gas 6. Slice off the hard root base of the radicchio and cut in half vertically. Cut out a V-shaped section to remove some of the thickness of the stem, then remove a couple of the central leaves to make a little well or platform on which to sit the cheese.

Mix together the dressing ingredients and rub into all the open leaves of the radicchio. Place each of the radicchio halves on a baking tray, cut side up, and flatten open the leaves a little. Take 2 of the figs and slice into quarters, then place 2 of the quarters cut side down on each of the radicchio heads and squash into the leaves. Top with a round of the goat's cheese.

Put the remaining 4 figs on the baking tray and put into the oven to bake for 25–30 minutes, until the cheese is melted, bubbly and a little golden and the radicchio is soft, the figs bursting with juice. Toast the cobnuts or hazelnuts in the same oven for 7 minutes until golden (rub off the bitter skin on regular hazelnuts) and roughly chop them. Slide each half of radicchio on to a small plate. Cut each fig in half and place around the radicchio heads. Make sure you gather up all the figgy juices to pour over each platter. Scatter with the chopped cobnuts or hazelnuts. Finish off with a seasoning of sea salt and black pepper and a further little dribble of olive oil if needed. Serve warm.

Wild Rice, Wild Mushrooms & Salted Walnuts

SERVES 4

200g mixed wild mushrooms
150g chestnut mushrooms
250g wild rice
50g butter
40g broken pale walnuts
2–3 large spring onions,
    finely sliced into rounds
120g baby spinach
a dash of Seville orange juice
    (or cider vinegar)
a handful of fresh parsley leaves,
    chopped

The stock
20g dried porcini mushrooms
650ml just-boiled water

The dressing
1½ tablespoons balsamic or
    elderberry vinegar (see page 259)
3 tablespoons olive oil
sea salt and black pepper

AUGUST TO OCTOBER FOR
WILD MUSHROOMS

I am quite boring about the virtues of wild mushroom hunting: crawling under low, face-scratching baby pines searching for the moment when a whisper of damp on the cheek and an imperceptible increase in warmth tells you there may be a cep close by pushing up through needles and moss; or spotting fragments of telltale creamy yellow chanterelle or hedgehog mushroom dotting the turf among bracken. The hunt is exciting and the taste worth the effort.

For those trapped by city and circumstance, it is still worth hunting down genuine wild mushrooms for this dish. The quantity needed won't prove more expensive than a block of good cheese or a portion of well-reared meat or well-caught fish.

Wild rice is not actually rice, but a grass seed still often gathered by hand. Full of nutrition (protein, amino acids), it combines its rugged nuttiness with soft mushrooms and buttered, salty walnuts for a bowlful of deliciousness. Not strictly in season, a dash of Seville orange juice is, however, perfect for adding a little extra acidity to the rice. Pull one out of the freezer to split for the occasion or substitute a drop or two of cider vinegar.

Soak the dried porcini in the hot water for at least 10 minutes – while you prepare the rest of the mushrooms. Strain out the mushroom pieces, reserving the soaking water. Give the porcini a rinse to remove any clinging grit, and squeeze dry.

Clean and prepare the wild mushrooms following the directions on page 241. Boil up the trimmings in the porcini soaking water and strain again in a sieve lined with kitchen paper.

Don't slice the mushrooms too finely for this dish – they should have scale and texture against the fine needle-y wild rice. Leave smaller caps whole, and tear or slice bigger caps into slightly smaller portions. Ceps should still be sliced thinly (2–3mm), but leave as much length as possible.

Wash the wild rice thoroughly in a sieve under a cold tap to flush out any dust. Place in a lidded pan with the mushroom stock and a pinch or two of salt. Bring to the boil and cook gently with the lid on for 30–35 minutes, until tender.

Cook the mushrooms, starting with fresh ceps, then field or chestnut mushrooms and finishing with chanterelles and the soaked porcini. Melt some of the butter over a medium heat in a largish pan, add the prepared fungi and toss around to coat with melted butter. It is likely the pan will get sticky with delicious buttery, mushroomy juices. Use a drop or two of water to deglaze and loosen these delicious flavours from time to time. The mushrooms will be cooked when they are soft and golden.

To toast the walnuts, rattle them around in a hot, dry pan until they become golden and release a toasted smell – around 5 minutes. Add a tiny amount of butter and some sea salt, allowing it to melt on the nuts for a minute or two more, then remove from the pan on to kitchen paper.

As the rice is approaching readiness, the pan should be almost dry. When just tender and starting to split, showing the whitish inside of the rice, drain through a sieve, then put the rice back into the warm pan to dry.

Pour the warm rice into a wide bowl and muddle through the sliced spring onions and baby spinach. The spinach will relax and soften in the heat of the rice but will retain green freshness. Dress the rice with the dressing. Squeeze over a little Seville orange juice or cider vinegar, then taste to check and add more if needed.

To finish, tip over the cooked mushrooms. Deglaze the mushroom pan a final time with a little drop of stock and pour over the rice. Scatter over the salty, toasted walnuts and the chopped parsley and serve warm, in wide bowls.

GATHER COOK FEAST

A Little about Wild Mushrooms

Foraging

It's not the purpose of this book to give comprehensive guidance on foraging for wild mushrooms, their habits, their edibility or otherwise, or important advice on avoiding poisonous species – for this you must educate yourself before venturing out into the woods.

There are many foraging courses available that teach identification, habitat and collection, and a wide variety of good books to support a growing interest (see Further Reading and Learning at the back of the book). You must develop a knowledge that goes deeper than a list of defining characteristics, and it takes time to build the familiarity required.

Make sure to use a basket for collection, to allow spores to scatter as you walk, perpetuating the crop in future years. In the same way use a knife to cut the caps free, to avoid damaging the important but delicate mycelium underground (the mycelium is an underground web of tendrils that form the 'body' of the fungi; the caps we see are the fruiting bodies only). Get in the habit of doing a spore print with your specimens when you get home – this can clinch correct identification between a few similar species.

Some Delicious Types

I tend to stick to a small variety of fungi I know very well and which grow around where I live – happily some of the most delicious. Chanterelle mushrooms are the first to appear in late summer (especially under bracken and at the mossy edge of a pinewood). The hedgehog mushroom is very similar, a pale apricot colour and possibly even more delicious than the chanterelle. In these years of silage production, field mushrooms are increasingly hard to find, but when you do they are wonderful, growing mysteriously on old pasture. It's hard to mistake the giant puffball, which can sometimes be found growing on the verges of major roads. Slice this huge cap into steaks and brown in plenty of butter with salt and pepper. The blewit is another tasty and beautiful mushroom. Once we found a patch in the dusk on Exmoor below a circle of pine trees among the remains of rocky field banks. But the prize find is, of course, the cep (or porcini in Italian). My mushroom-hunting friends guard the location of this king of mushrooms like state secrets – betray at your peril.

Cooking Wild Mushrooms

Finally, when a basket of foraged mushrooms sits on the table, here are some tips on how to deal with them. Never wash mushrooms – they are very absorbent and will sop up water like a sponge. Instead, clean them using a soft, dry pastry brush to remove any peat, pine needles or other gritty detritus, brushing delicately among the gills or pores. If the mushroom caps are very grubby, they can be wiped with a damp piece of kitchen paper. Trim off any dry or excessively dirty tips of the stem and any damaged, slug-eaten or mushy bits (you can boil these up in a little water for a few minutes and strain through kitchen paper to make an extra, valuable drop of mushroomy stock). If it has been wet on the day you collected, leave them out on a tray lined with kitchen paper to air-dry a little.

Chanterelles and hedgehogs are best torn lengthways into strips. Cap mushrooms such as field mushrooms, parasols and ceps are better sliced across the cap with a knife.

Wild mushrooms will often release a vast quantity of water once they are plunged into a hot pan, and you have to work through this stage in the cooking. Melt a little good butter in a hot pan, add the prepared mushrooms and cook for a few minutes. If the mushrooms do become wet, raise the heat to boil off the water, then add a little more butter to toast them to golden.

Chanterelle, hedgehog and parasol mushrooms will take around 5–10 minutes to cook; field mushrooms and blewits 10–15; and ceps benefit from a little longer cooking, 15–20 minutes.

When cooked to golden and meltingly tender, grind over some salt and pepper, throw a spoon or two of crème fraîche into the pan, stir around and then eat on a slice of hot, buttered sourdough toast.

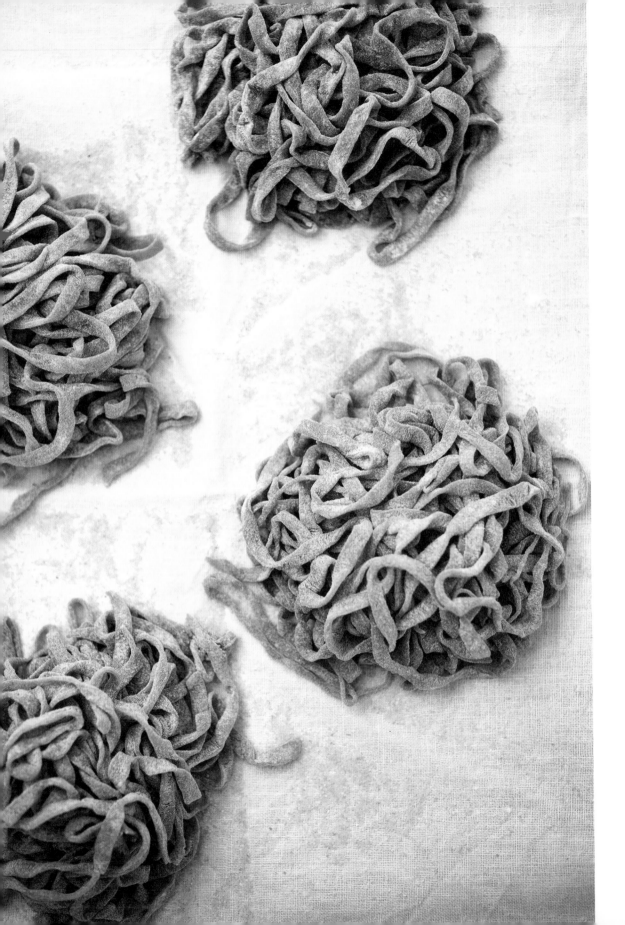

Chestnut Pasta with Blue Cheese & Sage

SERVES 8 AS A STARTER,
4–6 AS A MAIN COURSE

The pasta
200g fine-ground chestnut flour
200g pasta flour, plus extra
    for rolling
4 eggs
1 tablespoon olive oil
a good pinch of sea salt
semolina

The finished dish
150g butter
150g breadcrumbs, quite
    coarse and not too stale
sea salt and black pepper
leaves from 16 sprigs of fresh sage
    (about 64 leaves)
300g blue cheese, crumbled

This rich, nutty pasta is made from chestnut flour, which with blue cheese, breadcrumbs and sage makes for a really delicious autumn-day meal. Choose a creamy, easily crumble-able, strongish blue here – my preference is Stichelton, but it's not crucial.

This recipe makes enough to serve 4–6. If you are cooking for fewer, reduce the quantities or store the surplus well-dried pasta in a plastic ziplock bag or large jar to keep for a week or two.

The pasta
Sift the flours on to a clean work surface. Make a well in the middle and crack in the eggs. Add the olive oil and salt to the eggs and whisk.

Start incorporating the flour from around the edge to make a paste. Keep going until most of the flour has been mixed in, then switch to using your hands to bring everything together as a dough. If it feels dry, don't be tempted to add any water just yet (it's easy to go too far).

Knead the dough on the work surface for around 10 minutes until it is smooth and springy (don't skimp, it takes time). Only add a dribble of water if it stubbornly remains too dry, and if it's too wet add a sprinkle of pasta flour. Shape the dough into a neat block, wrap in clingfilm and set aside for 1 hour. You can make the pasta dough in advance and store it in the fridge for up to 2 days.

Prepare a series of baking trays lined with baking paper.

Unwrap the dough and divide into four portions. Keep three wrapped up while you roll the first. If you don't have a pasta machine, use a rolling pin and a sprinkle of pasta flour to roll the dough out as evenly and finely as you can (1–2mm). Then dust heavily with flour and roll up into a flattened scroll. Slice neatly across the scroll so as to divide the pasta into tagliatelle-shaped strips. Quickly unravel the strips before they stick to each other and transfer them to the lined baking tray.

If using a pasta machine, flatten the lump of pasta dough and feed it through the widest setting. Fold it in three (like a business letter) and feed it through again, placing one of the open ends into the rollers first so that all the trapped air is squeezed out. Repeat this process several times, until the pasta is coming out in a neat, smooth rectangle. Use a tiny sprinkle of flour to stop the dough sticking. Now feed the dough through each successive setting on the machine, until the dough is long and thin. Depending on your pasta machine, it may be best to stop one short of the finest setting if the pasta is becoming too fragile. Then lightly dust the dough with flour and divide into two pieces so it's easier to handle.

Feed one piece of dough through the tagliatelle attachment on the machine (or cut by hand into strips 6–8mm wide). Transfer the pasta strips to a lined baking tray, dusting them well with plenty of semolina. They can sit in a happy loose tangle. Repeat the rolling and cutting with the remaining piece of pasta dough. Leave out for at least an hour (and up to a day if you want it really dry for storage) to dry a little before continuing.

The finished dish

Melt half the butter in a large frying pan. A light pan is ideal, as it will be easier to toss. Add the breadcrumbs and a generous pinch of salt and brown over a medium heat, tossing or stirring regularly, until the crumbs are crispy. Transfer them to a bowl.

Bring a large pot of well-salted water to the boil. Shake the excess semolina off the pasta before you lower it into the pot and boil until al dente, about 3–6 minutes.

Meanwhile melt the other half of the butter in the same big frying pan and add the sage leaves. Soften over a medium-low heat, stirring occasionally, until they turn translucent green (not brown).

Save a mug of pasta cooking water, then drain the pasta in a colander. Add the pasta to the frying pan along with 120ml of the pasta water (about half a mug), the crumbled blue cheese and several grindings of black pepper. Toss everything together, keeping the pan over the heat, until the sage leaves are distributed, the cheese starts to melt and the water and butter emulsify into a sauce. Serve immediately, scattered with the fried breadcrumbs.

A Woodsy Braise

40g butter

10 small round shallots, peeled
but left whole

200g very thick smoked back bacon,
rind removed, cut into 2cm squares

200g flat portobello mushrooms,
wiped and sliced

600g waxy potatoes, scrubbed and cut
into large, thick, angular shards

4 good sprigs of fresh thyme

sea salt and black pepper

800ml vegetable or chicken stock

200g vacuum-packed cooked
chestnuts

250g green cabbage or kale,
washed, spun, stems or
cores removed, shredded

fresh marjoram leaves

truffle oil (optional)

60–100g Gorwydd Caerphilly

If braising is good for meat, it is also good for vegetables.

Here potatoes, bacon, mushrooms and chestnuts combine with cabbage and shavings of Caerphilly in a broth-filled bowl for a simple, early autumn supper.

Some vacuum-packed chestnuts disintegrate faster than others, so try to assess the firmness of the ones you have and adjust the time in the pan accordingly. The aim is to add them early enough to absorb the juices right to their chalky hearts, but not so early that they fall apart. And, if you can, find smoked bacon cut thick to 3–4mm to give a desirable substantial quality to the braise.

Find a very wide, lidded pan big enough to braise all the ingredients with plenty of room to spare. Melt the butter over a gentle heat and brown the shallots in the pan for 10–15 minutes – until they are becoming slightly soft and caramelized in places.

Add the bacon and mushrooms, turn up the heat a little, and toss them in the buttery pan for a further 5 minutes, until golden. Then add the potatoes and thyme and toss them in the pan juices for a minute or so, until they have softened at the edges. Season well with salt and pepper.

Add the stock and simmer, covered, for 7–10 minutes, then add the chestnuts and cook for a little while longer. When the potatoes are tender and the chestnuts have taken the juices to heart, add the cabbage for a few minutes until tender and incorporated, but still bright green. Remove from the heat and season with salt and pepper, as you will.

Serve in big bowls, with a little torn, fresh marjoram, perhaps some truffle oil and plenty of shavings of Caerphilly.

Bay & Bacon Wrapped Pork Fillet, Smoked Potatoes & Buttered Apples

SERVES 4

The wrapped pork
1 pork tenderloin (around 500g)
olive oil
sea salt and black pepper
12 slices of very thin, unsmoked
    streaky bacon, rind removed
20–25 fresh (not dried) bay leaves
150ml chicken stock
125ml Madeira
cider vinegar

The smoked potatoes
600g small Charlotte potatoes,
    scrubbed
sea salt
1 tablespoon olive oil
3 tablespoons apple wood dust

The buttered apples
a knob of butter
2 small tart eating apples, peeled,
    cored and chopped
sea salt and black pepper

This is a celebratory main course to share with friends on an autumn evening. They will arrive to find your home dreamily scented with sweet apple smoke like a woodland glade. The bacon and bay wrapping gives a savoury, hallowed quality to the tenderloin, which combines beautifully with the smoked potatoes. A small pile of sharp, buttery apple sits on the side and some long lengths of sweated, charred leek or pak choi will add colour.

Pat the pork dry with kitchen paper, brush it all over with olive oil, season with salt and pepper and leave to reach room temperature.

Boil the potatoes in salted water until just tender – around 15–20 minutes. Drain and allow them to dry off in the residual heat of the pan. Rub them with a little olive oil.

Following the instructions on page 227, smoke the potatoes using the apple wood dust for around 20 minutes. Leave room in the smoker for the vapours to circulate between the potatoes – work a couple of batches if necessary.

Heat the oven to 200°C/180°C fan/gas 6.

While the potatoes are smoking, prepare the pork. Line up all the slices of streaky bacon side by side (each overlapping the other a little) to make a big square sheet of rashers just longer than the length of the tenderloin. If it is much longer, overlap the slices a little more or take one or two slices away. Then cover the whole of the piece of fillet with the bay leaves – they should stick relatively easily to the slightly sticky oiled surface of the fillet. Lay the pork at right angles across the line of rashers – the ends of the rashers should poke out on either side of the loin. Then, one by one, plait the slices of bacon across and over the top of the tenderloin until completely covered.

Gently lift the pork into a small roasting tin just big enough to hold it. If you only have very big tins, improvise a nest of foil for the pork in the centre of your pan. Pour the stock around (it should just be a very shallow pool under the bacon), then place in the oven and cook

for 30 minutes. If you have a meat thermometer it will be done when the temperature reaches 65–70°C or when the pork is a tiny bit pink in the middle.

While the pork is cooking, make the buttered apples. Melt the butter in a non-stick pan, then add the apples and let them cook gently on a low heat until tender and golden. Season with salt and pepper.

In a small pan over a high heat, reduce the Madeira to half its volume, ready to make the sauce. Five minutes before the end of the cooking time, pour off the stock and pan juices from the meat, adding them to the Madeira pan, and reduce a little more to intensify. Season with a little pepper (you may not need salt) and add a dash of cider vinegar to brighten. Keep warm until you are ready to serve.

Once the pork is cooked, remove it from the oven and let it rest for a few minutes.

Unwrap the bacon and remove all the bay leaves, then slice the pork into rounds and arrange on hot plates with curls of bacon (if the bacon wasn't very thin it might need a few seconds in a hot pan to crisp it up), with the hot-smoked potatoes and buttered apples on the side.

Serve the reduced sauce in a warm jug to hand around.

Slow Roast Pork

SERVES 4 HUNGRY OR
6 ABSTEMIOUS PEOPLE

3 dried bay leaves, torn into pieces
2 teaspoons fennel seeds
1 teaspoon black peppercorns
3 teaspoons coarse salt
finely grated zest of 1 lemon
1.5kg piece of pork shoulder (off the
    bone, skin scored for crackling)
2 carrots, peeled and roughly chopped
2 onions, peeled and roughly chopped
2 sticks of celery, roughly chopped
cloves from 1 head of garlic,
    peeled and left whole
250ml white wine
250ml chicken stock

AVAILABLE YEAR ROUND,
BUT BEST IN THE AUTUMN
FROM SMALL SUPPLIERS

The shoulder is a hard-working part of the pig, but it becomes a delectable and juicy cut with generous time and a slow oven. After several hours of cooking it should be so tender you can cut and serve it with a spoon. Ask the butcher to score the skin for you, or do it yourself with a very sharp knife, taking care not to cut into the flesh beneath the layer of fat.

This dish goes very well with the spiced pickled quinces on page 254 and the salt-baked vegetables on page 187, or a rough mash of turnips with swede and some moist, buttered greens.

First make the spice rub. Grind the bay leaves, fennel, peppercorns and salt with a mortar and pestle to a fine powder. Mix in the lemon zest. Then rub the mixture over the pork, being sure to get it inside the scored skin. Set the pork aside for an hour to come to room temperature and take on the flavours of the rub.

Heat the oven to 240°C/220°C fan/gas 9.

Mix the carrots, onions, celery and garlic and spread over the base of a medium roasting tin. Place the pork on top, skin side up. Pour around the wine and stock and cover with a large tent of foil. Make sure the foil doesn't touch the pork, and seal it really well around the rim.

Roast until the liquid starts to steam and show signs of simmering, around 30–45 minutes (check by lifting up a corner of the foil and taking a peek). Reduce the temperature to 190°C/170°C fan/gas 5 and continue roasting, with the foil still in place, until the meat is meltingly tender. This will take 2–2½ hours – maybe even 3.

Remove the pork to a board and pour all the juices and vegetables into a big sieve set over a pan or bowl. Squish the soft vegetables against the sieve to encourage as much juice and vegetable pulp through as possible until nothing more will come out, then discard the pulp.

Heat the grill and position a rack below to accommodate the pork around 8cm below the element. Return the pork to the roasting tin and pour the sauce around the meat. Grill until the skin has crackled to your liking. Keep an eye on it, as a fierce grill can burn it easily. While the skin is crackling the sauce should be bubbling and reducing slightly. If you don't have a grill (as I don't in my Aga), you can opt to cut off the crackling and put it back into a very hot oven to crisp up. In this case reduce the sauce in a small pan. Wrap the joint well in foil and keep covered with a blanket to keep warm. Some juices will have seeped out of the joint while resting, so pour them back into the sauce – so as not to waste the flavour.

Use a knife to cut away and divide the crackling, then chop the pork up roughly and serve with pickled quince, mash and greens, making sure everyone gets plenty of sauce.

Spiced
Pickled Quince

MAKES 1 LARGE OR 2 SMALL JARS
(APPROX. 500ML TOTAL)

1 unwaxed lemon
500g quinces (4 small or 2–3 if
    large, see note on the right
    about wastage), fuzz washed off
350ml white wine vinegar
175g white granulated sugar
175g soft brown sugar
¼ teaspoon cloves
¼ teaspoon anise seeds
¼ teaspoon black peppercorns
¼ teaspoon allspice berries
½ teaspoon yellow mustard seeds
1 bay leaf
3 blades of mace
a 2cm piece of cinnamon stick
a pinch of sea salt

LATE SEPTEMBER TO
DECEMBER FOR QUINCE

It is hard to overstate the appeal of quince – beautifully photogenic, with a seductive, dreamy fragrance, they also slow-cook to a sticky delectability and a beautiful deep amber colour. This is a sweet-sour, sticky and spicy pickle, to serve with a good sharp Cheddar and crusty bread or with the slow roast pork on page 251.

Despite their beauty, the most flawless quinces can harbour damaged insides, so always buy a few more than you need to avoid coming up short. Quinces will keep for a month or two in a cool, dry place.

This is a small batch – enough for one jar. Multiply it up to make more. If you are making it to store, it is best to strain the spices out of the pickling liquid before pouring it into the jars, or the pickle will become too spicy. If making to use within a week or so, leave the spices in for dramatic effect. The choice of spices can be flexible to your taste or what you have in your cupboard, but always use whole spices.

Pare several strips of lemon zest from the lemon using a vegetable peeler.

Half fill a small saucepan with water and squeeze in the juice from the lemon. Peel the quinces, then cut them into quarters lengthways and add them to the pan. If they are very large you may want to divide each piece into two. (It's easier to remove the cores after they've cooked, as quinces are so hard.) Make sure there is enough water to just cover, then bring the pot to a gentle simmer and poach the quinces, covered, until tender – about 30 minutes.

Meanwhile in another saucepan heat the vinegar with the lemon zest, sugars, spices and salt, stirring to dissolve the sugar. Bring to the boil, then remove from the heat and allow the pickling liquid to infuse while the quinces finish cooking.

Lift the poached quinces out of their water and allow them to cool a little. Using a paring knife, take out the cores, taking care to remove all the hard grainy area around the core. Add the quinces to the pickling liquid and return to the heat. Simmer gently, uncovered, for between 30 minutes and 1 hour (depending on the size of the quince pieces), until the quinces are translucent, deep amber in colour and the liquid has become syrupy.

GATHER COOK FEAST

Sterilize one or two jars (see page 105) to piping hot and use a slotted spoon to transfer the quinces, using a teaspoon to ease them in snugly. Remove the bay leaf and cinnamon stick as you go. If the pickling liquid is still thin, you can now boil it hard for a few minutes to make it more syrupy, but don't let the jars cool down too much. Pour the syrup over the quinces to fill the jars and seal immediately. The unopened pickle will last for a year on the shelf – once opened, store in the fridge and use within a couple of weeks.

White Beans with Smoky Bacon

SERVES 2 AS A SIDE

Rich beans for alongside any roast meat, or with a salad. Any white bean will do, but the Asturian waxy Granja bean is the best because it has a waxier quality that pairs so well with meats.

Peel and finely chop a clove of garlic and sizzle in a hot pan with 1 tablespoon of olive oil. Add 40–50g of good, smoked streaky bacon in lardons or chopped rashers and cook until golden and the fat is starting to release. Add 350g of cooked white beans along with a little cooking water (100–150ml), a good glug of olive oil, a sprig or two of rosemary, and sea salt and black pepper to taste. Cook gently on a low heat for 30 minutes (keeping them moist with additional judicious applications of water if needed), until the beans are soft and their liquid starchy. Check the seasoning before serving.

Elderberry Vinegar

MAKES ABOUT 650ML

500g elderberries (about 20 big sprays)
500ml red wine vinegar
350g white granulated sugar

AUGUST TO SEPTEMBER FOR
ELDERBERRIES

This is so easy and so very delicious. Elderberries have a deep, slightly tannic, complex flavour that makes this vinegar very useful in the kitchen – for vinaigrettes on dark red or green salad leaves; to bolster meat pan sauces; to dribble into soups or stews as a finishing touch (like the autumn minestrone on page 223), or anywhere where you would use an aged balsamic vinegar. Or pour boiling water over a couple of tablespoons in a mug, with a little sugar, to make a surprisingly delicious and soothing drink. The berries are also very nutritious, having high quantities of vitamin C, A and antioxidants. Raspberry or blackberry vinegar can be made in the same way.

Pick elderberries that are deep wine-red to purple and plump, after any traces of green have disappeared and before they start to wither. Avoid trees next to busy roads and fields that may have been sprayed.

Wash and dry the sprays of elderberries. Remove the berries by rubbing with the fingers as if making pastry. This removes ripe berries and leaves behind the green ones firmly attached to the stalk. Measure around 500g of berries into a lidded container and partially crush them with a fork or potato masher to get the juices flowing. Add the vinegar, mix and cover. Leave the mixture to macerate at room temperature for 5 days, giving it a shake every time you remember.

Sterilize a bottle (see page 105) until piping hot. Strain the vinegar through a sieve lined with clean, damp muslin. Once it has drained, gather up the muslin and squeeze to extract as much juice as possible. Pour the liquid into a medium saucepan with the sugar and heat to dissolve, stirring occasionally. Now bring it to a boil and boil hard for 10 minutes uncovered. This sterilizes the mixture and will reduce it slightly.

Using a funnel, pour the hot vinegar into the hot bottle, leaving a 1cm gap at the top. Put the cap on and turn the bottle upside down to sterilize the insides of the lid. (Note: If you only half fill a bottle, leave it uncovered until it has cooled completely, otherwise the trapped air will expand as it heats and can cause the bottle to explode.)

Store the vinegar somewhere cool and dark and use within a year.

Two Crab Apple Jellies

MAKES 3 X 450G JARS

For crab apple & bay
1kg crab apples, halved,
    stalks removed
1.5 litres water
10–12 large fresh bay leaves
a pinch of sea salt
around 1kg white granulated sugar
around 6–8 tablespoons cider vinegar

For crab apple & rowanberries
1kg mixed crab apples and
    rowanberries (at least half
    must be crab apples)
1.5 litres water
a pinch of sea salt
around 1kg white granulated sugar
around 6–8 tablespoons cider vinegar

AUGUST TO SEPTEMBER FOR CRAB
APPLES AND ROWANBERRIES

Any crab apple based jelly is very useful to pull out of the cupboard for spooning alongside cold meat or cheese; or with slices of crackling roast pork (and many other roast meats) or with the mutton baked in hay on page 309.

Here are two pale jewel-pink jellies to choose between – the first a sweet-savoury one with bay and the second with rowanberries adding a tangy bitterness, perfect alongside a slice or two of sweetly complex venison. You may find stalks have a firm grip – halve the crabs first to pull out slightly sideways.

Crab Apple & Bay

Place the crab apples and water in a saucepan. Add the bay leaves, crumpling them to release their flavour. Bring to the boil, then simmer, partially covered, for around 1 hour, until the apples are soft.

Strain the mixture through a scalded jelly bag, or a large sieve lined with damp muslin. Let it drip for several hours. Resist the temptation to squish the bag (it will make the jelly cloudy).

Place several saucers in the freezer to chill, and sterilize three clean jam jars (instructions on page 105).

Measure the strained apple juice, then pour it into a preserving pan and set over a medium heat. Add a pinch of salt and then add 200g of sugar for every 250ml of juice. Let the sugar dissolve slowly, stirring occasionally. Now bring the mixture to the boil and after a few minutes add 1 tablespoon of cider vinegar for every 200ml of juice.

Boil hard until setting point, resisting the urge to stir too often. The bubbles will become smaller and slower and the mix will start to run off the spoon like syrup. To test for setting point, pour a teaspoon of syrup on to a chilled saucer and let it cool down completely. Push across the puddle with a finger: the jelly should form a skin and wrinkle up. If not, continue boiling for another few minutes then test again. A jam thermometer helps you know when the setting point is approaching (look for 104°C), but the saucer test is still wise.

GATHER COOK FEAST

Turn the heat off and skim off any scum forming on the surface with a metal spoon. Bring out the tray of hot jars from the oven and use a heatproof jug or ladle to carefully fill them with the hot syrup, almost to the very brim. Seal immediately and leave to cool. The unopened jelly will last for a year on the shelf – once opened, store in the fridge and use within a couple of weeks.

Crab Apple & Rowanberries

Wash, spin dry and strip the rowanberries from their stalks. Halve and de-stem the crab apples. Place the apples, rowanberries and water in a pan. Then follow the method above, leaving out the bay leaves.

Pickled Damsons

500g damsons

4 blades of mace

3 cloves

1 stick of cinnamon, split into
    large chunks

a good thumb-sized piece of
    ginger, split lengthways
    into 8 segments

300ml inexpensive balsamic vinegar

200ml good red wine vinegar

200g sugar

a pinch of sea salt

zest of ½ a lemon, shaved with a
    vegetable peeler into long curls

zest of ½ an orange, shaved with a
    vegetable peeler into long curls

LATE AUGUST TO SEPTEMBER
FOR DAMSONS

Aged eight, skinning my knees on the green limbs of our family damson tree and stretching precariously to find that one last, tender damson, before pitching it into the pink plastic wastebasket strapped to my waist … this love goes deep. Damsons are one of my favourite fruits – a beautiful soft grey-blue bloom on a black-purple fruit and an intense flavour, which needs sugar to shine.

They are one of the few remaining truly seasonal fruits, appearing for a short time in September, making the most delicious jam, but wonderful in fools and ice creams and also very good pickled to eat with cold meats in mid-winter. If you can resist the urge to pillage, keep them as long as possible before opening because the almondy flavour of the damson stones will better permeate the liquor. Make only what you truly think you will need and make it again fresh next year.

This recipe will also serve for morello cherries or wild plums.

Prepare the damsons by picking off all the stalks and leaves, then rinsing and drying with a clean tea towel. Prick the skin of each damson a few times with a clean pin: this prevents them slipping out of their skins.

Sterilize four jars (instructions on page 105).

Put all the spices, vinegar, sugar and salt into a stainless steel pan and bring to the boil. Simmer for 15 minutes, then pour through a sieve to extract the spices. Set aside to cool.

Layer the damsons, zests and spices attractively in each sterilized jar. Then top up with the spiced vinegar until the damsons are completely covered. Screw the lids on tightly, wipe the outside of the jars free from dribbles and store for at least 1 month before eating. The damsons should last through the winter, but discard if any mould appears.

Plum & Walnut Tart

MAKES 1 X 23 OR 25CM
TART TO SERVE 8–10

The pastry
180g plain flour
60g caster sugar
a pinch of sea salt
120g cold unsalted butter,
    cut into cubes
finely grated zest of 1 lemon
1 egg, lightly beaten with a fork

The filling
100g walnut pieces
50g Demerara sugar,
    plus extra for sprinkling
1 rounded tablespoon plain flour
a pinch of sea salt
rounded ½ teaspoon freshly
    ground anise seeds
50g soft unsalted butter
1 egg
500–600g plums, halved and
    stoned, or quartered if large

AUGUST TO SEPTEMBER FOR PLUMS

A stunning, richly fruity tart for sharing – juicy, caramelized plums meld into a soft walnut paste. The pastry is tender but sweet and delicious with a nutty quality. The anise seeds are similar in taste but different from star anise and have a delicate aniseed taste more suitable for sweet recipes.

To make the dough, mix the flour, caster sugar and salt in a bowl. Add the butter and lemon zest and rub together with your fingertips until it resembles breadcrumbs. Mix in a dribble of egg – just enough to be able to bring the dough together. You won't need all the egg: save the rest for brushing the base of the baked tart shell. Briefly work the dough to bring it together into a ball. Wrap tightly in clingfilm, flatten into a disc and chill for at least 1 hour in the fridge, until very firm.

Lightly flour the work surface and roll out the chilled dough into a circle and to an even thickness of 3mm. Rotate the dough frequently and use more flour as needed to ensure it does not stick. Carefully lay the pastry in the tart tin and press it into shape. If the tender pastry falls apart as you line the tin, don't worry; just squish the broken pieces together in the tin. It will firm as it chills in the fridge and be fine once baked. Trim off the excess pastry, but leave a margin sticking up above the rim by a couple of millimetres to compensate for oven-shrinkage. Chill for at least 30 minutes in the fridge.

Heat the oven to 200°C/180°C fan/gas 6. Prick the base of the tart shell several times with a fork, line with a square of baking parchment and fill with baking beans. Bake for around 20 minutes in the lower half of the oven, until cooked through. Remove the paper and beans and return to the oven for 5 more minutes until the base is golden. Now brush the base with the reserved egg and return to the oven for a couple of minutes to ensure the egg cooks and creates a seal. Let the tart shell cool.

Spread the nuts over a small baking tray and toast in the oven for 8–10 minutes, until golden and fragrant. Tip them into a tea towel, then gather it up around the nuts and rub vigorously to loosen the skins. Pick out the pieces of nut and don't worry if they're not all perfectly skinned. Let the nuts cool, then whizz them in a food processor together with the

Demerara sugar, flour, salt and anise seeds until they resemble fine sand. Add the softened butter and egg and process again until smooth.

Spread the walnut filling inside the tart shell. Arrange the plums cut side up over the filling, closely packed, and sprinkle them with a little Demerara sugar. If the pastry has taken enough colour in the first baking you may want to protect the edges by folding narrow lengths of foil over the exposed edges, secured around the belly of the tin with string – a bit fiddly, but worth it for the perfect tart. Place the tart on a baking tray and return it to the oven, this time on the top shelf, for around 40 minutes, until the plums have caramelized. It may still be a little loose in the centre but once it cools on a rack it should have firmed to a soft set. Wait until cool before removing from the base to serve.

Hazelnut &
Honey Ice Cream

SERVES 4

160g toasted, skinned hazelnuts
100g caster sugar
1 good tablespoon honey
    (around 30g)
4 egg yolks
175ml full cream milk
175ml double cream
a pinch of sea salt

The hazel was one of the first small trees to re-colonize the British Isles after the last Ice Age. This magical, delicate tree has provided nuts for eating since then.

Combine the deep nuttiness of roasted hazelnuts with the warmth and floral notes of a good local honey and these two ancient flavours can reconnect us with tastes our ancestors would recognize. Choose a light or medium mixed wildflower or clover honey, rather than (otherwise wonderful) jelly-like heather or intense chestnut – both of which could overwhelm the hazels.

On a more practical modern note, I often buy ready roasted hazelnuts. To make ice cream without an ice cream maker, see the instructions on page 112.

Blast the skinned, toasted hazelnuts and the caster sugar in a food processor for around 3–4 minutes, until the nuts have formed a thick paste. You may need to stop the mixer a few times during this process and scrape the nut mixture down off the sides of the bowl.

Add the honey and egg yolks to the food processor and mix for a further 2 minutes. Then gradually add the milk, cream and salt and mix again, ensuring everything is well combined.

Churn in an ice cream maker, according to the manufacturer's recommendations, until done. Scoop out into a plastic container and freeze.

Slow Roast Quince

SERVES 8

4 large, fat quinces
    (plus spare in case of damage)
8 cloves
around 300g white granulated sugar
around 300ml water
1 stick of cinnamon
juice of ½ a lemon
clotted cream, thick cream
    or very thick yoghurt
ground, chopped or flaked nuts
    (walnuts, almonds, hazelnuts
    or pistachios), to finish

LATE SEPTEMBER TO
DECEMBER FOR QUINCE

These treasures will take patience and a long, slow oven to reveal their full, sticky, delectable glory. The quince only appears in the late autumn in Turkish shops or specialist markets. If you have problems finding quince, use one of the sources at the back of this book.

Heat the oven to 160°C/140°C fan/gas 3.

Wash the fuzz off the quinces, then peel, halve and core. Don't throw the cores and skins away just yet. You will need a very sharp little knife to excavate the fibrous and hard parts of the core. Shape a neat bowl-shaped hollow to safely contain the liquids. If they will not sit flat, slice a tiny sliver off the underside to create a base. Arrange snugly in a roasting tin or ovenproof pan just big enough to hold them. They will be browning by now, but it's OK – this will go when they cook.

Put a clove in each quince's hollow and then spoon 2–3 tablespoons of sugar on to each quince, filling the hollow copiously. Pour a mug of water into the pan; add the cinnamon stick, around 5 quince seeds and several peelings of quince skin to the water to deepen the colour. Add the lemon juice too.

Cover with a lid or foil and bake in the centre of the low oven for 4 or more hours, until the quinces are deep red and turning translucent and the syrup is thick. You will need to check the quinces hourly. First they will become tender, then golden, later developing a tinge of red and finally a deep, rich, amber-red. Each time you check them, turn them gently and baste them liberally to keep them moist and cooking evenly. Also, check the consistency of the syrup and top up with water if it becomes too thick (it will set solidly on cooling if it goes too far). The syrup should be the consistency of oil rather than something like runny honey.

Once the quinces have achieved their glorious colour and the syrup is on the slightly thicker side of the oil spectrum, they are done. Allow them to cool in their syrup. Serve at room temperature, with some of the sticky syrup poured over and topped with clotted cream and ground, chopped or flaked nuts – walnuts, almonds, hazelnuts and pistachios are all good.

GATHER COOK FEAST

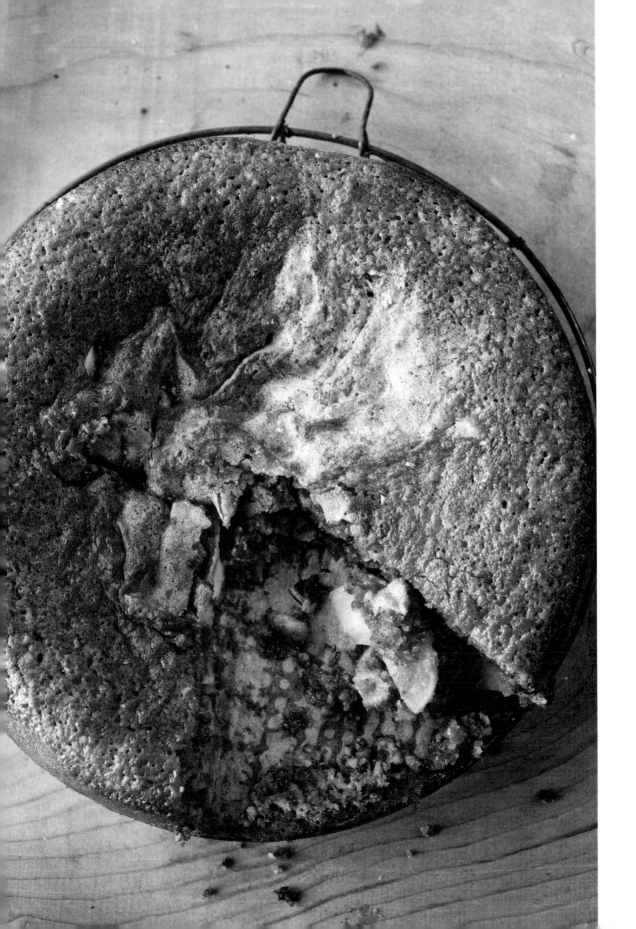

Walnut & Apple
Soft Cake

MAKES A 20CM CAKE

150g walnuts

2 large apples

a little lemon juice

2 eggs

225g golden caster sugar

a pinch of sea salt

100g butter

150ml full cream milk

100g plain flour, sieved

3 teaspoons baking powder

Fragrant apples and toasted walnuts join together in a warm cake with a soft, melting heart. The apples sink beautifully into the loose mixture, poking their pale backs out like so many diving whales, tender beneath. Serve little pieces, just warm, at the end of a meal, perhaps with a few pale walnuts on the side. Or keep for a morning cup of coffee.

Look for pale, fresh walnuts: many are sold far too old, dark and bitter. Use the most flavoursome apples you can find; delve into the wonders of Worcester Pearmain, Blenheim Orange, Egremont Russet or Cox's Orange Pippin. Slice these eaters more finely than delicious cookers like Bramley or Howgate Wonder, which you can also use, but which soften more in cooking.

Heat the oven to 200°C/180°C fan/gas 6. Line a 20 x 7cm round cake tin (with removable base) with baking paper.

Grind 75g of the walnuts in a food processor until they resemble rough sandy crumbs. Then toast the remaining 75g of walnuts on a baking tray in the oven for 3–5 minutes, until they just give off a toasted smell and before they take too much colour – they should be just turning golden. Rub them briskly in a clean tea towel to remove as much of the skins as you can. Pick out all the pieces of walnut, leaving behind the skins, and scrunch any whole nuts into smaller pieces.

Peel, quarter and core the apples. Slice each quarter lengthways, not quite all the way through to the tip. They should be just joined, but able to be spread out like a fan shape of very fine slices. Dribble with a little lemon juice to stop them browning while you make the batter.

Whisk the eggs and 200g of the sugar with the pinch of salt until the mixture becomes thick and forms trails. Melt the butter in the milk over a medium heat until nearly boiling and add to the egg mixture, stirring all the time.

Fold in first the sieved flour and baking powder and then the ground walnuts, spoon by spoon. Try to work quickly and use as few cuts and folds as possible to keep all the lightness in the cake. Choosing a rubber spatula or metal spoon for the task will keep in vital air.

Pour the liquid batter into the prepared tin. Work fast (batter will be working already) to fan out the pieces of apple and push them down, core edge first, into the batter, arranging and spreading as much as you can. Scatter the toasted walnuts over the surface. Sprinkle the remaining caster sugar over the top of the apple-studded batter.

Bake for 20–30 minutes, checking after 20 minutes for signs of done-ness. The cake should be light golden, all wobble gone, but still with a shadow of vulnerability.

Cool on a rack to just warm or leave to cool for eating later.

WINTRY   FLINTY
EXPOSED   WILD BIRDS
SCATTER   DARK
BITTERS   UPLAND
KALE   CRAG MUTTON
TUSSOCK   THORN

JUNIPER   COLD   PINE
HAY BLANKET   SPICE
LIQUORICE   GOLD
FIRELIGHT   WARMING

Outside my Japanese ryokan window is a noisy, fast-flowing river. It's a sliding window and it took me a while to figure out how to open it, but once I did, the smell of night poured in – musty intense pine; a sort of peaty smell; fresh mountain air with a whiff of wood smoke. Being liberated from the drudge of the city – the fumes of cars, the constant low-grade humming activity – is energizing. Some people love mountains and some don't. I am definitely in the former category. Any follower of Toast may notice a possibly wearisome frequency of mountain pictures.

Much of our upland landscape is a product of farming practice, either for sheep or game birds. What is considered wild and beautiful is often over-grazed and consequently species-poor. There is now only just over 1% of ancient upland habitat left in Britain, much of it woodland and much of that in Scotland. But some strides are being made to restore upland habitats (Rewilding Britain, the charity founded by George Monbiot, is working to bring parties together around this issue).

This is a controversial topic – the value of traditional upland farming culture versus biodiversity. Moreover, upland grazed sheep have a flavour unmatched by lowland beasts: mutton and hogget in particular. So, in response and musing on complexity, we roasted mutton in hay to bring a flavour of moorland to the plate and created a frisky broth to drive off winter blues.

A week spent in Scotland in the early weeks of writing this book was the perfect place to work on some of the recipes. I walked in the mountains and gathered pine branches to make into pine jelly to eat alongside venison, my favourite winter meat.

We also made liquorice chocolate pots. Liquorice is interesting. Its root has been grown in Pontefract since the eighteenth century. In this area Pontefract cakes and liquorice allsorts had their origin, starting a localized confectionery industry. Liquorice has an intensely sweet anise flavour that combines beautifully with chocolate, but has uses beyond: with spices as a rub for pigeon or game; with juniper, as flavouring for venison; as a delicious ice cream; or to pair with rhubarb in a sponge cake.

Winter is also a time of year for sausages. Try making your own smoked venison versions with the project in this section. They are easier than you may imagine and deeply gratifying to make, while outside successive storms blow dead leaves away.

Dark Lentil Soup with Horseradish Cream & Browned Butter Leeks

SERVES 4 AS A SMALL BOWL
OR 2 VERY HUNGRY PEOPLE

1½ tablespoons olive oil
1 clove of garlic, peeled and sliced
1 small red onion, peeled and sliced
2 purple heritage carrots,
    peeled and chopped into
    chunky sticks (1 x 3–4cm)
1 stick of celery, trimmed and chopped
    into chunky sticks (1 x 3–4cm)
200g dark green lentils,
    washed and drained
500ml mushroom stock (see page 224)
500ml vegetable stock
1 dried or fresh bay leaf
a couple of sprigs of fresh thyme
1–2 teaspoons tomato purée
smoked sea salt and black pepper
3–4 teaspoons finely grated
    fresh horseradish root
3 tablespoons crème fraîche
a small squeeze of Seville
    orange juice (optional)
35g salted butter
8–10 medium slices of the white
    or pale green part of a leek

Little dark green lentils have a mineral look to them – green and grey-ly mottled like the rocks of gabbro or peridotite. Using dark carrots and onions strengthens the theme: the soup becomes like a deep cave of rich earthy flavour, with a clean kick of horseradish cream and a caramelized application of leeks browned in butter on top.

Smoked sea salt is a fairly new arrival, but it works well here. Unsmoked would do fine too. Seville oranges are included as an optional extra – quite a pain to rush out just for that – but if you have some in your freezer or waiting for a marmalade session, squeeze a little juice to finish the soup.

Purple heritage carrots are often found in farmers' markets or specialist suppliers nowadays. They have a good flavour and a less watery body. The soup will taste similar made with any self-respecting orange carrot, but it will look less special.

In a largish, lidded pan heat the olive oil and gently soften the garlic and the red onion until just transparent – about 5 minutes. Then add the carrots and celery, and stir around until slightly softened – 5 minutes more.

Add the drained lentils and stir in the oily mixture. Pour over the mushroom stock and 300ml of the vegetable stock, tuck in the herbs and bring to the boil. Cover and continue to boil gently, adding additional vegetable stock if needed to keep a good soupy consistency, for around 1 hour, until the lentils are soft and tender (they may be tender earlier, but gentle, long cooking will create the necessary soupy texture). Halfway through the cooking, add the tomato purée and season with smoked sea salt and black pepper.

Mix 3 teaspoons of horseradish with the crème fraîche, stirring to create a loose texture. Taste to assess the punch of the horseradish and add more if you like.

Once the soup is ready, add a squeeze or two of Seville orange juice (if you have some to hand), then taste to check the seasoning and adjust. Mash a few of the lentils against the side of the pan to thicken the broth. Keep warm while you brown the leeks.

DARK LENTIL SOUP WITH
HORSERADISH CREAM & BROWNED
BUTTER LEEKS / CONTINUED

Melt the butter in a frying pan and add the leeks. Stir around to coat them in the butter, then pour off the excess butter into a little container. Brown the leek slices on either side in the now drier, hot pan until golden and tender (they will fall apart but this doesn't matter). Remove from the pan. Add the butter back and heat until the colour starts to change to pale brown. Remove from the heat immediately.

Assemble the soup bowls thus – add the portion of lentil soup, create a little pool of the horseradish cream in the centre, arrange the browned leeks over and then dribble over the browned butter to serve.

Mutton Broth with Warm Spices

SERVES 4–6

The broth
1–1.5kg mutton bones
4.5 litres cold water
5 fat cloves of garlic, unpeeled
2 onions, unpeeled
8cm piece of ginger, unpeeled
1 star anise
2 black cardamom pods,
   cracked open
5cm piece of cinnamon stick
6 cloves

The soup
100g pearl barley, rinsed
   twice in cold water
450g mixed diced winter
   vegetables (carrot, swede, turnip,
   potato, celeriac, celery, parsnip)
8–10 button mushrooms, quartered
2 teaspoons Demerara sugar,
   or to taste
5 teaspoons Asian fish sauce,
   or to taste
sea salt
2 handfuls (around 100g) of
   finely shredded Savoy cabbage
1 or 2 fresh red chillies, deseeded
   and finely sliced
2 spring onions, finely sliced
   on an angle
leaves from a small bunch
   of fresh mint
1 lime, cut into wedges

When I first started putting together the recipe list for this book, I was quite strongly in favour of using all British produce. But as I read more widely, I questioned what actually is British food? As waves of influence have flooded these islands by trading or invasion, so the mix of produce has flexed and changed with fashion and time. And spices first arrived with the Romans.

In this recipe the idea of a Scottish mutton and barley soup is combined with classic pho spices: mutton is well able to handle the ginger and spice. If you don't have a cast-iron pan for charring the vegetables, use the flames of a gas burner, or a tray under a hot grill. If you don't have black cardamom, leave it out. Start this soup a day ahead.

Put the bones into a large stockpot and cover with the cold water. Slowly bring to the boil and cook for 10 minutes (skimming off the scum). Then heat a flat-bottomed cast-iron pan over a high heat and use it to char the garlic, onions and ginger, turning frequently. After around 10 minutes they should be covered with black patches, beginning to soften and smelling fantastic. Cool, then peel away most of their papery skins. They don't need to be perfect.

Roughly chop the onions and finely slice the ginger. Add the onions, ginger, garlic, star anise, black cardamom, cinnamon and cloves to the stockpot. Turn down the heat and simmer uncovered, very gently, for 5 hours.

Strain the broth. Pick out any nice-looking pieces of meat and add them to the broth. There should be around 2 litres of stock.

Chill the broth overnight, then remove the solidified fat. Pour it into a saucepan and add the pearl barley. Cover and simmer for 10 minutes. Add the diced vegetables, mushrooms, sugar, fish sauce and a small pinch of salt to the pot, then cover and simmer for another 20 minutes, until the vegetables are tender. Add the cabbage and half the chillies and continue simmering for 5 minutes, to soften the cabbage. Taste and add more salt, fish sauce or sugar if you think it needs it.

Serve piping hot, sprinkled with the spring onions, mint and the rest of the chillies, and with lime wedges to squeeze.

Mountain
Cabbage Soup

1 onion, peeled and finely diced

25g butter

100g pancetta, finely diced

a good pinch of chilli flakes

4 anchovy fillets

1 bay leaf

leaves from 2 good sprigs
   of fresh thyme

4–6 large slices of stale sourdough
   wheat bread (depending on size)

1 clove of garlic, peeled
   and left whole

½ a big head of green cabbage,
   preferably Savoy, quartered,
   cored and thickly sliced

sea salt and black pepper

200g Ogleshield or similar, grated

100g Parmesan, finely grated

1 litre chicken or beef stock

WINTER FOR SAVOY CABBAGE

Our mountains may be lower than in the Val d'Aosta in Italy where this soup originates, but we do have bleak moors, dark forests and bitter, wet winter days. This soup is welcome after just such a day: warming, heart-filling and sustaining.

A mountain cheese that melts well is important, softening into the cabbage and bread. In the Alps it would be something like Fontina, Comté, Gruyère or Abondance. British candidates could be Mayfield, a sweet fruity semi-hard cheese from Sussex with natural holes, like Emmental; or Ogleshield, a washed rind cheese from Somerset with a fruity, wine-like flavour and good melting properties. If you have a grill, press it into service at the end to bubble and brown the cheesy top.

In a medium-sized heavy-based casserole pot, soften the onion in the butter over a medium heat for about 4 minutes. Add the pancetta and continue cooking for another 5–6 minutes, stirring often. Add the chilli flakes, anchovies, bay leaf and thyme and continue until the onion is completely soft, the anchovies have disintegrated and the pancetta is just starting to caramelize – about 10 minutes.

While all this is happening, toast the bread. Rub it on both sides with the garlic while it's still warm.

Add the cabbage to the pot, turn up the heat and cook until it starts to wilt, tossing it frequently for 4–5 minutes. Remove the contents of the pot to a bowl.

Now create layers in the pot. Place half the toast in the bottom, tearing it into pieces so it fits well but is not closely packed, with gaps for juices to collect. Spread over half the cabbage mix, and season with salt and plenty of black pepper. Spread over half of each cheese. Now repeat all the layers, ending with the remaining grated cheese.

Pour over the stock and top up with water if needed so that the ingredients are just submerged. Partially cover and cook at a gentle simmer for 20–30 minutes, until the cabbage is completely tender. Finish under the grill if you like, to brown the top. Ladle immediately into large bowls, piping hot.

Jerusalem Artichoke Crisps

MAKES 1 BOWLFUL

Delicious, oven-baked crisps for nibbling with a drink or adding to a winter salad.

Scrub around 200g of knobbly Jerusalem artichokes and slice them very finely. Toss the slices in a little olive oil and sea salt and arrange them on a baking tray, making sure they are one layer thick and don't overlap.

Bake them in the oven at 200°C/180°C fan/gas 6 for 20–25 minutes – by which time they should be lightly toasted at the edges but still pale in the middle. Remove from the oven to cool, using a slice to free them from the surface of the tray.

Raw Root Salad

SERVES 4

1 small parsnip
1 medium white turnip
100g piece of celeriac
100g piece of swede
1 medium carrot
1 medium beetroot
1 tablespoon white sesame
   seeds, toasted
a small handful of fresh parsley
   leaves, shredded
2 small fresh red or green chillies,
   deseeded and chopped

The dressing
1 tablespoon rice vinegar
1 tablespoon mirin or rice wine
2 tablespoons sesame oil
a good squeeze of orange juice
1 teaspoon sugar
1 clove of garlic, peeled and crushed
1cm piece of ginger, peeled
   and grated
sea salt and black pepper

This is a clean, healthful, crunchy salad for mid-winter and is surprisingly sweet. If you favour some vegetables more than others, do feel free to alter the proportions. It can absolutely be adjusted to your taste.

Key to the success of this salad is the right size of shaving. The best level is the coarsest grate in the food processor, which makes something like a fine, bendy matchstick. Don't be wooed into using a hand grater, which will produce a sloppier mix more like coleslaw, which isn't at all the intention. If you don't have a food processor, then fine slicing with a knife, plus appropriate levels of mindfulness for the task, works on many levels too.

Peel all the vegetables and cut into equal-sized pieces small enough to fit through the opening in the lid of your food processor. Grate all the vegetables using the coarsest disc on the food processor, starting with the white ones and moving to the carrot afterwards. Remove these to a big bowl, then grate the beetroot into the empty mixer bowl.

Whisk the dressing ingredients in a small jug with a fork and pour over the white vegetables and the carrot, gently lifting to mix the colours and distribute the dressing. Do this without messing with it too much. Then add the beetroot and carefully riddle it through the other colours – you want to achieve a good mix without allowing the beetroot to stain the other root colours too much. It should look prettily speckled.

Leave the salad to stand for 10 minutes or so, to absorb the dressing. Finally, sprinkle the sesame seeds, parsley and chillies over the top.

Kale, Roast Vegetable & Barley Salad

SERVES 4

2 small parsnips

2 medium carrots

1 medium beetroot

100g piece of celeriac

1 banana shallot, peeled
and sliced

1 tablespoon olive oil

sea salt and black pepper

4–5 baby leeks, split along
their length

125g pearl barley

200g curly kale

juice of ½ a lemon

4 fresh Medjool dates, sliced

50g Parmesan, finely grated

The dressing

2 tablespoons lemon juice

5 tablespoons olive oil

a good grinding of sea salt
and black pepper

This is a really hearty salad that combines a kick of nutrients from the raw kale, with soothing barley and roast vegetables. It is important to strip the kale from its stalks and chop it really finely, then massage with lemon to break down the cellulose in the leaves and bring out its green sweetness.

Eat this salad for lunch on any day (and especially after feasting the day before). Its combination of nutrient-rich foods will restore flagging spirits. Scatter with Jerusalem artichoke crisps (see page 285) if you like.

Heat the oven to 220°C/200°C fan/gas 7.

Peel all the root vegetables and chop into 2cm pieces, then scatter over a baking tray with the sliced shallot. Toss with the olive oil and season with a good grinding of salt and pepper.

Put the tray into the hot oven and roast for 30–45 minutes, until the veggies are soft and slightly caramelized at the edges. Add the split leeks to the baking tray for the last 20 minutes.

Rinse the pearl barley well in a couple of changes of water, then boil it in fresh water for 30 minutes until tender. Drain well and leave in the warm pan to dry off until you are ready for it.

Wash the kale and strip the stalks. Using a good sharp knife, shred the kale by slicing it very finely this way and that, until you have achieved a fineness near to chopped parsley. Put it into a bowl and squeeze over the juice of half a lemon, massaging it well into the kale leaves by hand to break down and soften the fibres. Leave for at least 20 minutes before assembling the salad.

Once the barley and the vegetables are cooked, mix them into the kale together with the sliced dates, and toss with the dressing, then the grated Parmesan.

Serve warm, scattering with Jerusalem artichoke crisps if you will.

GATHER COOK FEAST

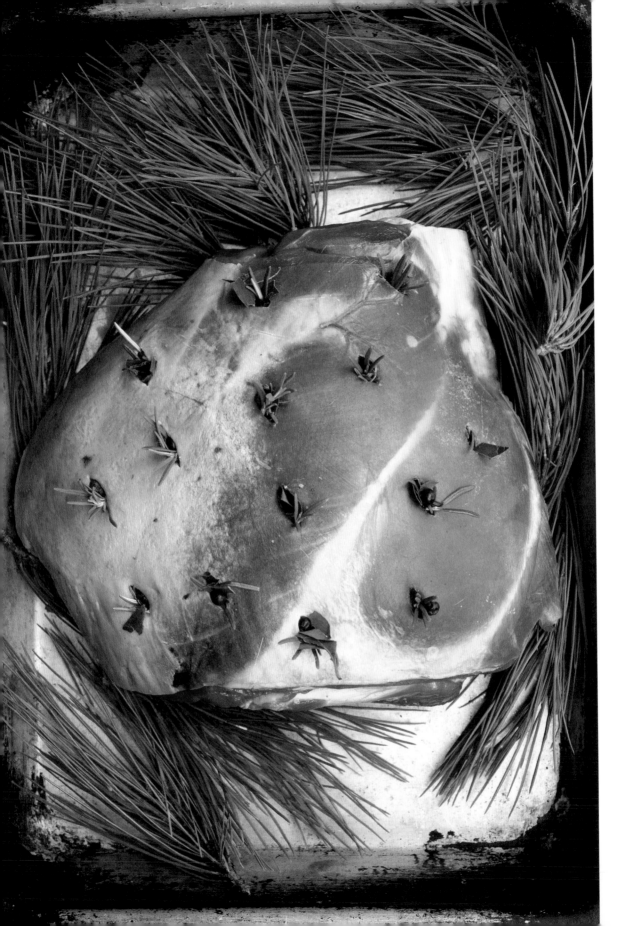

Juniper Roast Venison
with Pine Jelly

3kg haunch of venison, with bone in
12–14 juniper berries, slightly crushed
3 good sprigs of fresh rosemary
4–6 fresh bay leaves, sliced
    into shards
olive oil
sea salt and black pepper
10 slices of streaky bacon
small branches of Scots pine
    or Norway spruce

The sauce
150ml red wine
250ml chicken stock
1 tablespoon redcurrant jelly or
    crab apple jelly (see page 260)
1–2 teaspoons Worcestershire sauce
a dash of elderberry vinegar
    (see page 259) (optional)
sea salt and black pepper

LATE OCTOBER TO MARCH
FOR WILD VENISON

A simply roasted haunch of venison, fragrant with juniper berries and paired with a delicate pine jelly, is lighter and less work than turkey or goose for Christmas and feels like a breath of moorland on a plate.

Venison is a lean meat and many recipes try to compensate for the lack of fat by using marinades, basting and larding with fat. Instead, try roasting the meat with less intervention, fast and hard, as you would lamb. The result was a delicious revelation, but is only suitable for younger tender meat. For more mature animals, braising or stewing is a better option.

Investing in a probe meat thermometer is really worthwhile – if you want medium rare you can guarantee medium rare. The pine jelly (see page 295) needs to be prepared ahead. The crab apple jelly and elderberry vinegar are on pages 260 and 259 respectively.

Take the venison out of the fridge in good time so that the meat is at room temperature before you begin roasting. It will take about an hour, but you can prep it while you wait.

Using a sharp knife, make 12–14 slits at approximately 2–4cm spaces all over the top of the haunch. Into each of these holes push a juniper berry, a couple of spiky leaves of rosemary and a shard of bay. Dribble a little olive oil over the surface, season with salt and black pepper, then drape over the streaky bacon to cover the haunch completely.

Heat the oven to 220°C/200°C fan/gas 7. Cover the base of your roasting tin with the pine branches and nestle the haunch in the centre. Transfer the roasting tin to the oven for 30 minutes.

After 30 minutes, reduce the temperature to 190°C/170°C fan/gas 5 and roast for a further 12 minutes per 500g for medium rare or 10–12 minutes for rare. If you use a meat thermometer, the meat will be done when it reaches 55°C for rare and 60°C for medium rare. But you will need to take it from the oven when it's 5°C below, because the temperature will continue to rise as it is resting.

When the meat is done, remove from the oven and place on a large plate. Cover first with a copious tent of foil and then an old blanket or towel to keep it warm while you make the sauce.

JUNIPER ROAST VENISON
WITH PINE JELLY / CONTINUED

Skim off any fat from the roasting tin and place the tin over a low heat. Gradually pour in the wine, stirring all the time to combine with the meat juices. Then add the stock, redcurrant jelly and Worcestershire sauce, boiling fast to remove the raw wine flavour, reducing and intensifying to a good savoury hit – around 15 minutes. Taste the sauce and season with salt and pepper, tweaking the flavour to suit by adding a little more jelly or Worcestershire sauce. A dash of elderberry vinegar at the end gives the sauce a little lift. Add the juices from the meat, boil it up one final time and decant to a waiting hot jug.

Remove the coat of streaky bacon and discard. Carve into thinnish slices and serve with slow-baked salsify and scorched Brussels sprouts (see page 296), with the sauce and pine jelly (see opposite) to hand around.

Pine Jelly

MAKES 500ML – A LARGE JAR

100g Norway spruce or Scots pine
    needles, stripped from the branch
500ml boiling water
250g caster sugar
10g gelatine leaves
1 tablespoon lemon juice

Expert forager Miles Irving recommends three conifer needles for cooking: Norway spruce, Scots pine and Douglas fir. I have tried the first two. Norway spruce is the classic Christmas tree, with the advantage of providing decoration and contributing to lunch, but the needles are small, so stripping takes some time. The taste is delicate, woodsy and subtly of Christmas itself. Scots pine needles are much larger and it's easier to strip the required quantity. The taste is rounder and has a more lingering fragrance. Both are lovely. Collect good fresh branches, away from dusty roads. Use secateurs for a clean cut and minimal tree damage.

Steep the needles in just-boiled water for 18–24 hours.

The next day, drain through a sieve lined with muslin to exclude both needles and needle dust. You should have a clear, pale green liquid.

In a pan over a medium heat, warm the liquid with the sugar until it all dissolves. While the liquid is heating, steep the gelatine leaves in a dish of cold water until flexible. Then lift out the gelatine leaves and squeeze away excess water. Add the gelatine leaves to the warm pine syrup and stir thoroughly until the gelatine is dissolved (do not boil – it makes the gelatine stringy).

Finally add the lemon juice. Cool the syrup over a dish of iced water, then pour into a sterilized, lidded jar (see page 105).

Keeps in the fridge for up to 1 week.

Scorched Brussels Sprouts

SERVES 2–4

For supper with pieces of shaved, crumbly Lancashire cheese on top. Or with any game or roast meats.

Heat your oven to 240°C/220°C fan/gas 9. Remove any battered outer leaves from 300g of Brussels sprouts and trim the base to a clean finish. Slice in half lengthways and place on a small baking tray, tossed with a little olive oil, sea salt and black pepper, spreading them out into a single layer. Roast them in the oven for 15–20 minutes, until a little charred at the edges, tender and still juicy (check and turn them around halfway). Serve with a squeeze of lemon juice if you like.

ALL WINTER FOR SPROUTS

Flowering Sprouty Tops with Mustard Dressing

SERVES 4

The year turns, a little more light comes and the sprouting tops start to grow. Pick them fast and eat them for lunch. Make this with any late winter flowering top: the very tip of Brussels sprouts, purple sprouting broccoli or flowering tops of kale. Only the tenderest need apply.

Whisk 1 tablespoon each of lemon juice and white wine vinegar together with 4 tablespoons of good olive oil, 3 peeled and very finely chopped cloves of garlic and 3 tablespoons of Dijon mustard. Season with sea salt and black pepper. Add a pinch or two of caster sugar if the dressing is a little sharp. Stir or shake really well to create a thick emulsified dressing.

Cook 400g of sprouting tops in boiling salted water for 2–3 minutes (the time will depend on how fresh the tops are), until tender. Drain the tops through a colander and pop it back on the hot pan to dry off for a moment or two.

JANUARY TO MARCH
FOR FLOWERING TOPS

Then toss the tops in a large bowl together with the mustardy dressing.

GATHER COOK FEAST

Pheasant Breasts
with Quince Purée

SERVES 6

3 quinces, peeled and quartered
    but not cored
juice of 1 lemon
6–8 tablespoons caster sugar
sea salt and black pepper
a small dash of olive or sunflower oil
6 skinless pheasant breasts
    (each weighing around 100g)
90ml Marsala
1 litre good pheasant or
    chicken stock

SEPTEMBER TO FEBRUARY FOR
FRESH PHEASANT, LATE SEPTEMBER
TO DECEMBER FOR QUINCE

Delicious pheasant breasts with quince purée – good with buttery mashed potatoes and wilted spinach or curly kale.

Put the quinces into a saucepan with their peel and half the lemon juice, and cover with cold water. Put the lid on and simmer until the quinces are completely tender but still holding their shape – about 30 minutes.

Use a slotted spoon to lift out the quince quarters and carefully cut out their cores (easier now the quinces are cooked). Take care to remove all the hard grains surrounding the core too (you can return the cores to the cooking water and use it for making the quince jelly opposite).

Immediately cut the quince pieces into small cubes and purée together until smooth, with 6 tablespoons of caster sugar, a pinch of salt and a small dash of lemon juice, using a jug or stick blender or a food processor. Taste and add more sugar if it needs it.

Heat the oven to 220°C/200°C fan/gas 7. Warm a dash of oil in a frying pan over a high heat. When the pan is really hot, add the pheasant breasts and sear for a couple of minutes on each side until nicely browned but nowhere near cooked through. Remove to a baking tray or roasting tin and let them rest for 15 minutes.

Reduce the heat under the pan and deglaze with the Marsala. When the wine has reached a good syrupy consistency, add the stock and boil really hard until reduced by at least two-thirds and thickened to a really flavourful gravy (don't skimp on the reduction, this is where real flavour is developed – if in doubt taste and reduce more).

Finish the pheasant breasts in the oven. For medium rare, they will need 4–6 minutes, depending on their size. Gently heat the quince purée in a small pan.

Let the pheasant rest again for a few minutes, tented with foil, then cut each breast into thin slices on an angle against the grain of the flesh. Place a spoonful of quince purée on each plate and arrange the pheasant slices on top, spooning a little gravy over.

Quince Jelly

FOR 1 OR MORE JARS OF JELLY

Make this fragrant, fruity jelly using the boiling liquid, peels and cores left from making the quince purée on page 298.

Boil the quince poaching liquid, along with the peels and cores, for another half an hour or more, covered. The colour should intensify. Strain the quince liquid, measure it and pour into a large pan. For every 250ml of liquid, add 200g of granulated white sugar. Heat gently until the sugar has all dissolved. Then boil hard until the syrup reaches setting point. To test this, pour a teaspoonful of syrup on to a chilled saucer and let it cool. It should form a skin that wrinkles when pushed. If not, boil the syrup for longer and test again. Carefully pour the hot syrup into hot sterilized jars (see page 105) almost to the brim, and seal.

Pheasants with Apple & Cider

SERVES 4

a brace of pheasants (each
    weighing around 700g), plucked,
    drawn and ready for the oven
sea salt and black pepper
a small bunch of fresh thyme
3 Cox's apples, quartered and cored
160g lardons
12 small round shallots,
    peeled and halved
2 bay leaves, fresh if possible
25g butter
100ml Calvados or Somerset
    Cider Brandy
250ml dry cider
250ml good-quality pheasant
    or chicken stock

SEPTEMBER TO FEBRUARY
FOR FRESH PHEASANTS

The pheasant lives most of its life free in nature, at liberty to nibble and peck at weed and seed (as well as being fed at crucial times of the year). Its flesh is delicious and rich and is now on the slab sooner and less well hung than in the past: more palatable to many. Early in the autumn, when the birds are young and tender, you can get away with less liquid in the pot, but by mid-winter the rangier, older pheasants will need the full quantity of stock and cider. The leftover carcass can be used to make a game stock – useful for pheasant with quince purée (see page 298) – and wherever you need a chicken broth.

Pairing apples with pheasant is a classic combination. A mound of buttery mashed potatoes and the apples alongside bring the plate to completion along with some green cabbage, kale or Brussels (see recipes on pages 302 and 296).

Heat the oven to 200°C/180°C fan/gas 6. Season the pheasants all over with salt and pepper. Put half the thyme and one quarter of apple inside each pheasant's cavity. Choose a medium-sized casserole pot in which the pheasants will fit snugly. Use it to soften the lardons over a low heat until the fat starts to render – about 5 minutes. Add the shallots and continue for another 10 minutes until the shallots and lardons are caramelizing nicely. Add the bay leaves and fry for a further minute, then use a slotted spoon to transfer everything to a bowl.

Add the butter to the pot and let it melt over a low to medium heat. Add the pheasants and brown them for a few minutes on each side until golden. Put the lardons, shallots and bay leaves back into the pot and let them fall around the pheasants. Tuck in the remaining apple pieces.

Increase the heat to high and pour over the Calvados (letting it flame if you like, with the lid at the ready to suppress if needed). Now add the cider and stock. The liquid should come around two-thirds of the way up the pheasants. Bring everything to a bubble, then transfer to the oven, uncovered. Braise for 30 minutes or until the pheasants' legs move easily in their sockets when wiggled. Remove the pot from the oven and let it sit for 10 minutes. Lift the pheasants out and cut off the legs and breasts. Return the legs and breasts to the pot and serve with mountains of mashed potatoes.

Charred Winter Cabbage with Raisins

SERVES 4

400g dark leaves of winter cabbage, washed, drained and finely shredded

120g raisins

2 tablespoons sherry

2 tablespoons olive oil

2 tablespoons soy sauce

A rich and charred version of winter cabbage, good with roasted meats or stews. I sometimes eat this just on its own, too – when I feel like the umami hit of soy, the bitter hit of charred-ness and the minerals of deep green cabbage.

It can be made with any dark cabbage – Savoy cabbage, January King, curly kale and cavolo nero are all good – but make sure to use predominantly dark leaves and strip out tough stalks and scrappy bits.

Choose an Amontillado for soaking the raisins, though any sherry on the richer side of the curve would be good – the raisins are not going to blossom in their juicy best with a dry Fino or Manzanilla.

Serve this cabbage with deep rich meat such as the venison on page 293 or the pheasants with apple and cider on page 301.

First, make sure the cabbage is very well drained. If it is too wet it will not crisp properly. If in doubt, pile it into the centre of a clean, dry tea towel and pat it dry.

Soak the raisins in the sherry and top up with warm water to just cover. Set aside for 20–30 minutes, until the raisins have absorbed the sherry and are plump and juicy.

Heat the olive oil in a heavy lidded pan on a very high heat until it reaches the shimmering state just before smoking point. Throw the drained cabbage into the pan, where it will sizzle and sputter quite energetically. Do not be alarmed; this is what makes the delicious charring happen. Press the surface of the cabbage down to make good contact on the base of the pan, working around the whole surface. After around 2 minutes, use the spatula to lift up the edges and when you can see a good quantity of charred, but not burnt, cabbage, start to toss and mix it all together and cover with the lid. Lower the heat and allow the cabbage to steam in its own moistness for a couple more minutes.

Drain the raisins and squeeze out their liquor.

When the cabbage is tender, toss in the soy and the raisins and serve on a big warm platter.

A Dish of Baked Artichoke & Salsify with Mountain Cheese

SERVES 4

300g potatoes
600g Jerusalem artichokes
300g salsify
2 tablespoons olive oil
250g smoked pork lardons
2 red onions, peeled and
 thickly sliced
2 cloves of garlic, peeled and
 very finely chopped
150ml white wine
black pepper
400g Reblochon, Vacherin
 or Gubbeen
80g crème fraîche
20g Parmesan, very finely grated

NOVEMBER TO FEBRUARY FOR
JERUSALEM ARTICHOKES, OCTOBER
TO MARCH FOR SALSIFY

You would imagine the staple of the mountainside tartiflette to have an ancient past – but no! Reblochon cheese makers created it in the 1980s to promote sales of this pasture-rich Haute-Savoie cheese. This is an alternative made with some of my favourite deep winter root vegetables, properly seasonal with a sweet nuttiness.

The flavour of salsify is variously described as a cross between artichoke and celeriac, a mix of parsnip and asparagus, or a kind of vegetable oyster. However described, the flavour is delicate, a little earthy and vegetal. It comes in two types, the deep black scorzonera or the paler true salsify, both looking like a lifeless bunch of sticks, but peel it and a clear white root will emerge.

Good, thick, smoky lardons from heritage breeds will make a real difference to this dish, so it is worth searching them out.

A glass of white wine and a simple, bitter salad will go well.

Wash and peel the spuds, artichokes and salsify. Cut the potatoes and artichokes into even sizes and the salsify into sticks and plop them straight into a generously filled pan of salted water. Bring to the boil and cook until tender. When cooked, drain, cut into thick slices and dry off in the warm pan.

Heat the oven to 200°C/180°C fan/gas 6. While the vegetables are cooking, warm the olive oil in a pan, add the lardons, onions and garlic and soften well (covered) over a medium heat for 5 minutes. Remove the lid for a further 10 minutes. When the mixture is sticky and golden, add the white wine and boil hard for 5 minutes. Add the slices of artichoke, potato and salsify to the pan, turning with a spoon to coat them until it's all sticky and glorious, and the roots are starting to take a little colour (don't leave it so long that they disintegrate). Taste and add a grind of black pepper (it shouldn't need salt if the cooking water was well salted, and the cheese will add to the savour).

Layer half the mixture in a shallow baking dish. Slice (or spoon in the case of Vacherin) half the cheese on top, then lay in the rest of the mixture. Finish with another layer of cheese, some spoons of crème fraîche and a grating of Parmesan. Bake in the oven for 30–40 minutes, until bubbling and golden.

Roast Partridge with Smoky Lentils & Damsons

SERVES 2

1 carrot, peeled and chopped

1 stick of celery, sliced

2 shallots, peeled and sliced

1 tablespoon olive oil

2 slices of well-smoked streaky
    bacon, chopped

100g Puy lentils

2 bay leaves

2 sprigs of fresh rosemary

2–4 fresh sage leaves

350ml vegetable stock

smoked sea salt (or unsmoked)

250g damsons

40g sugar

2 partridges, cleaned

sea salt and black pepper

2 tablespoons sunflower oil

2–3 tablespoons red wine

SEPTEMBER TO FEBRUARY
FOR PARTRIDGE, LATE AUGUST
TO SEPTEMBER FOR DAMSONS

Once the skies turn a lowering grey and night arrives at half past four, my thoughts turn to partridge – that family-minded habitué of upland moors that, when disturbed by walking boots, rattles away in groups over the heather like so many mechanical toys. The whitish, wild meat is delicious, fed as it is by seeds, herbs and insects.

The smoky lentils give a rich, earthy accompaniment – the damsons a sharpness to offset the sweet flesh of the bird. Freeze a few damsons to extend the season. One partridge is a perfect portion size.

In a heavy pan, soften the vegetables in the olive oil for around 3 minutes, until translucent, then add the smoky bacon. Continue to cook until the bacon becomes opaque but not seared. Add the lentils, herbs and stock and gently simmer over a medium heat for 30–40 minutes. Add a pinch of smoked sea salt to the lentil pot halfway through the cooking. You are aiming for tender and just dry lentils.

While the lentils are cooking, prepare the damsons. Wash and dry the damsons and cut the flesh off the stones. Put them into a pan with the sugar and around 50ml of water. Cook over a low heat for 3–4 minutes until soft, then set aside for later.

Heat the oven to 200°C/180°C fan/gas 6. Clean inside the partridges with kitchen paper, remove any last feather ends, and season with salt and pepper inside and out. Heat the sunflower oil in an ovenproof heavy pan big enough to hold the partridges. Put the birds into the hot pan and cook first on one side, then on the other, then on the breast, then on the back – turning them every 3–4 minutes until nicely browned all over.

Put the partridges into the oven in their pan and cook for a further 10–15 minutes. Test for doneness by inserting a knife into the leg – it should be a little pink, but not bloody. When done, take the birds out and leave them to rest for 4–5 minutes. Deglaze the pan with a little red wine, stirring and boiling fast to release all the juices and soften the wine taste.

Serve with a little dark buttered cabbage or cavolo nero, with the lentils and warm damson sauce on the side. Pour the pan juices over the top of the birds.

GATHER COOK FEAST

Mutton Roast in Hay

SERVES 6–10, DEPENDING
ON THE SIZE OF THE LEG

a good handful of fresh herbs –
    thyme, parsley, rosemary
    and marjoram
sea salt and black pepper
6–8 anchovy fillets, chopped
2–3 large cloves of garlic,
    peeled and chopped
50g butter, at room temperature,
    chopped into small cubes
2–3kg leg of mutton, leg bone in
around 200–300g feeding
    meadow hay

The beans
2 or 3 x 400g tins of flageolet
    beans (depending on the
    weight of the mutton)
2–6 cloves of garlic, peeled and halved
a few sprigs of fresh rosemary
2–6 tablespoons olive oil

ALL WINTER FOR MUTTON

To nestle a piece of meat among dry grass to cook seems counter-intuitive, against habit, weird ... and yet, at the same time, strangely right. This is a fabulous way to cook a piece of meat: the hay insulates the leg of mutton, preserving moisture; the fat drips down on to the bed of hay, which absorbs it brilliantly; the vapours are able to circulate around the mutton, leaving the joint moist, not at all fatty, with a flavour sweetly reminiscent of the hay loft. Look for joints of deep colour.

A dish of moist, unctuous flageolet beans and a wilted green alongside are all that is needed.

Find hay in pet shops, choosing a feeding quality of a good, pale green colour, not dusty or mildewed. Quality is important, because the hay makes a real contribution to the flavour. If you are zealous and have a patch of long grass, you could cut your own in the summer and lay it out in the sun to dry, turning it over a series of sunny days, until it is dry to the touch. Store in a dry place.

Strip all the herb leaves off the stalks and chop finely with a grinding of sea salt. Mash the herbs, together with the chopped anchovies and garlic, into the butter until it forms a thick paste. Add a generous grinding of salt and black pepper.

Smear the paste all over the leg of mutton, covering it completely. Then make slits about 3cm wide all over the top and, with your finger, poke more of the butter mixture inside the joint for maximum infusion. If you have time, leave the joint to marinate in its coat in the fridge overnight. Otherwise, leave it for at least an hour.

Heat the oven to 200°C/180°C fan/gas 6.

Line the base of a large roasting tin with a good depth of hay, around 5–6cm. Place the leg of mutton on top of the hay and cover with the same quantity of hay on top. Finish off with a double layer of foil, making sure you tuck any stray bits of hay underneath the foil.

Place in the oven and roast for 30 minutes per 500g. Check for done-ness by piercing with a skewer. The colour of the juices will let you know the state of play inside the joint. The meat is medium rare when very slightly bloody juices flow out, and well done when clear juice flows out, so keep checking because ovens vary enormously. A probe thermometer will help accuracy – look for around 50°C for rare, 55°C for medium rare, 60°C for well done, remembering that the temperature will rise a further 5°C or so while the meat is resting.

While the meat is cooking, put the flageolet beans into an ovenproof dish together with their liquid, the garlic, a grinding of salt and pepper and a few small sprigs of rosemary. Pour the olive oil over the top of the beans (the amount needed will depend on the size of your dish but there should be a very fine slick over all) and place at the bottom of the oven for the last 30 minutes, until the flavours are combined and the dish is bubbling.

When the meat is done, remove it from the oven and set aside to rest for 10–15 minutes.

When you are ready, peel off the foil and the hay blanket and dust off all the little bits of hay that are left on the joint. There is no need to be too fussy. Slice the meat and serve.

Smoked Venison Sausages

MAKES ABOUT 8 SAUSAGES

700g minced venison shoulder

300g minced pork belly
   or scraps of pork fat

25g pure fine sea salt

2 teaspoons brown sugar

2 teaspoons black pepper

½ teaspoon ground mace

½ teaspoon ground juniper

½ teaspoon ground allspice

⅛ teaspoon chilli flakes or cayenne

1½ teaspoons dried sage or very
   finely chopped fresh sage leaves

finely grated zest of ¼ of an orange

3 cloves of garlic, peeled and
   very finely chopped

100ml red wine

1 spool of hog casings, soaked in
   cold water for an hour

LATE OCTOBER TO MARCH
FOR WILD VENISON

Sausages are easy to make. When you enquire into the contents of many sausages, you discover that they include proprietary flavouring mixes as well as rusk and other less enticing ingredients. How much better to make your own, control the ingredients and enjoy the process? Ask your butcher for the scraps of pork fat required (they may even provide the hog casings if they make their own good sausages (as mine did for nothing), or you can buy them online (see sources, page 336). If you have a mincer or a mincer attachment, sausage stuffer kits are cheap and easy to buy – if not, improvise using a large kitchen funnel with a generous nozzle.

These sausages are good both smoked and plain. Finish them under a grill or in a pan, to eat simply with a pile of mash and greens, or with the piccalilli veggies on page 315.

Combine all the ingredients except the wine and the casings. Mix everything together, then add the wine and massage well with your hands. Fry a little patty of the paste and taste to check the balance of seasonings – adjust if needed.

Put the end of the casings over the spout of the sausage stuffer or the funnel nozzle, bunching them up until they all fit (you will need around 2 metres in length).

Load the paste into the sausage stuffer or funnel, and prepare to make the sausages. You will make 8 sausages around 14–16cm long and 3–4cm thick.

Using a stuffer

Position a sloping board under the stuffer to take the emerging sausages. Pull around 10cm of the hog casings off the stuffer nozzle and turn the crank to force the meat into the casing, and the sausage should start to form with some gentle coaxing. Try to fill the casings as compactly as possible without bursting them. Gently hold your hand underneath each one as it emerges. Leave a 4cm length of casing between them for twisting later. As each is formed, turn the string of sausages a few times to twist the casing, making a neat division between each sausage.

Using a funnel

The method is similar but in this case use a flat board and hold the funnel over it. Pull around 10cm of casing off the nozzle and, using the handle of a wooden spoon or similar, force the meat down the nozzle to fill the casing. Using your fingers, squeeze the meat along the length of the casing to form an evenly sized sausage. Continue in this way until you have used all the meat.

Check the twists between each sausage, trim and tie the ends with string, then prick the ends with a clean pin – about 10 pricks per sausage. Spread over a tray and leave uncovered in the fridge for a couple of days to dry and start curing, turning them over after 24 hours.

Set up your stovetop hot-smoker and, following the instructions on page 227, smoke the sausages for around 30 minutes, until cooked and tinged brown with smoke. Cool, then store until needed. They'll keep in the fridge for 4 days or in the freezer for several months.

Smoked Venison Sausages
with Piccalilli Veggies

SERVES 4

1 small cauliflower, tough stem
  and outer leaves removed
2 teaspoons coriander seeds
2 teaspoons cumin seeds
1 tablespoon yellow mustard seeds
4 teaspoons ground turmeric
3 teaspoons yellow mustard powder
3 tablespoons olive oil
4 banana shallots, peeled
  and left whole
1 large courgette, chopped
  into thick rounds
400g mixed carrots, turnips
  and potatoes, peeled and
  chopped into small chunks
200ml vegetable stock
8 smoked venison sausages
  (see page 312)
4 tablespoons cider vinegar
1 teaspoon runny honey
300ml crème fraîche
sea salt and black pepper
a handful of baby spinach, washed
  and spun dry, ripped into pieces
a small handful of fresh parsley,
  chopped

Such a cheerful combination, bright yellow pickle-spiced vegetables accompanying dark and rich smoky sausages – for a moment in the year when you may be in need of some tangy heat on a gloomy day. The recipe for the sausages is on page 312. Smoked are delicious, but any good sausage will work.

Prepare the cauliflower by splitting it in half, making a 'V' to remove some of the central stem, then split into large florets (smaller ones will disintegrate) and slice the tender inner leaves.

Grind the whole spices into a powder in a pestle and mortar or spice mill. Add the powdered spices to the mix.

In a large, heavy lidded pan warm the olive oil and brown the shallots on all sides until golden – 2–3 minutes. Add the spices to the pan and toast for a minute more, then add all the prepared veggies and toss around in the spicy oil until glistening.

Add the stock, then cover and steam-cook over a low heat for 15–20 minutes until just tender.

While the vegetables are cooking, brown the sausages under a moderate grill or in a frying pan over a medium heat. Raw sausages need at least 15 minutes; previously hot-smoked sausages may need only 10. Either way, make sure the sausages are nicely browned on the outside and piping hot to their core.

Once the veggies are tender the stock should have mostly evaporated – if not, take the lid off and drive off the moisture. Add the cider vinegar, honey and then the crème fraîche. Gently stir around to combine (don't break the florets of cauliflower). Taste and season with salt and pepper or adjust the brightness with a little more vinegar if needed.

Muddle through the baby spinach and parsley to finish. Allow these to wilt a touch in the heat, then serve on hot plates with the sausages alongside.

Liquorice
Chocolate Pots

90ml full cream milk

100ml double cream

1 scant tablespoon caster sugar

a small pinch of fine sea salt

½ level teaspoon raw liquorice powder

4 teaspoons Scotch whisky

150g good-quality 70% dark
    chocolate, very finely chopped

double cream, to serve (optional)

Strong, dark and intense little pots of chocolate with a hint of sweet root liquorice.

Liquorice root has been grown on this island since monastic times. The root is naturally very sweet, although impractical to use for these purposes. More convenient is raw liquorice powder, which can be harder to track down. There are many uses for the powder, savoury as well as sweet. It has a fennel or anise-like flavour which savours cucumber, game, rhubarb or gingerbread. Choose a whisky partner here that is smooth and sweet rather than peaty in order to allow the liquorice to shine.

Heat the milk, cream, sugar, salt and liquorice in a small saucepan over a low heat so that it slowly comes to a gentle boil, stirring occasionally to help the sugar and liquorice dissolve.

As soon as the cream boils, stir in the whisky, then pour it over the finely chopped chocolate in a bowl or jug and leave for 1 minute without stirring. Then stir the mix to combine, starting in the middle and working outwards until it is completely smooth. Divide between four small cups or glasses.

Let the mixture cool at room temperature for 2 hours, then cover and transfer to the fridge to firm up.

Remove from the fridge half an hour before serving, with a little cream poured over the top if you like.

Gilded Gingerbread with Gorwydd Caerphilly Cheese

SERVES 9–10

150g bottled stem ginger

a little plain flour

250g self-raising white flour

1 teaspoon bicarbonate of soda

4 teaspoons ground ginger

1 teaspoon ground cinnamon

1 teaspoon ground mixed spice

300ml full cream milk

120g soft brown sugar

125g butter, plus some to
grease the tin

100g molasses

2–3cm piece of fresh root
ginger, peeled and grated

60ml ginger syrup, from
the ginger jar

120g golden syrup

1 egg, beaten

a pinch of sea salt

400g Gorwydd Caerphilly,
for sectioning into sticks

9 leaves of edible gold leaf
(50 x 50mm)

We made two large, square gilded gingerbread cakes for my daughter Rachel's country wedding and laid them alongside a wedding-cake tier of three successively sized Gorwydd cheeses. The dark glow of gold on the treacly brown of the gingerbread together with the chalky, mushroomy grey of the cheeses made a properly lavish centrepiece. The sticky, punchy gingerbread, together with the yielding softness of Gorwydd, was symbolically another marriage made in heaven.

I have to confess partiality here. The Trethowans, who make the excellent Gorwydd, are good friends of mine. They make their cheese with obsessive attention to its quality and, as a consequence, it is an unparalleled example of the clean, slightly salty/lemony Caerphilly taste.

Covering the gingerbread completely with edible gold leaf is quite expensive, but it's an indulgence that works for a landmark celebration. For lesser occasions, there are a couple of options – either use gold leaf, but don't cover entirely (a chequerboard can work well), or use a sprinkling of edible gold dust. The gingerbread will be delicious undecorated too.

This cake is even better in the days following baking.

Heat the oven to 200°C/180°C fan/gas 6. Grease and line a square, removable base 18 x 8cm cake tin with baking paper.

Prepare the stem ginger by chopping into 1–1.5cm cubes. Rinse, dry and dust with a little plain flour to prevent it sinking into the cake mix.

In a large bowl, sift the flour together with the bicarbonate of soda, the ground ginger and the spices.

Heat the milk in a saucepan and add the sugar, butter, molasses, root ginger, ginger syrup and golden syrup and stir until everything has melted into the milk. Remove from the heat. Cool to blood heat.

Make a well in the centre of the dry ingredients and pour in a little of the liquid. With a wooden spoon work your way around the bowl, pulling some of the flour into the centre, and start to mix the flour into the liquid. Once the first batch is mixed, continue to add liquid until all the flour is incorporated. When you have finished you should have a sloppy cake mix. Thoroughly beat the egg and a pinch of salt into this mixture. Scrape all the mixture out of the bowl and into the cake tin. The batter should end up around 5cm deep in the tin. Finally add the stem ginger to the mix, distributing it gently and evenly over the top. It will look like it's floating, but it may gradually sink to the bottom while in the oven.

Place the tin in the oven for 10 minutes, then reduce the temperature to 170°C/150°C fan/gas 3 and continue to bake for a further 30–45 minutes. Because cooking qualities vary so much from oven to oven, keep an eye on the cake during the cooking. You want it to be gently firm to the delicate touch of a finger; a skewer should come out clean. The gingerbread is best kept for a day or so to mature. Wrap in foil once cool to keep moist.

The decoration
The nine pieces of gold leaf will make a 15 x 15cm square of gold centred on the cake with a little gap around the edge. Gold leaf usually comes in folded paper wallets that make it easier to work with the featherlight pieces. There are two ways to apply it and both work equally well.

The first way is to open the paper fold and turn it upside down so that the gold leaf is face down over the cake (surface tension will tend to make the leaf stick to the paper for just long enough for you to manoeuvre it to the right position). Press the leaf down on to the cake so it adheres, then peel off the paper. Brush the surface of the leaf with a pastry brush or clean paintbrush so that it firmly sticks to the cake. Continue in this way until the entire surface of the cake is covered.

The second way is to use tweezers to peel the leaf from the paper and position it over the cake. Now brush the surface of the leaf to stick it to the cake in the same way. Either of these methods work, but don't get too hung up on perfection – the luxurious effect of the gold will far outshine any broken bits, overlaps or tiny gaps that may happen during the process. Serve a slice of the gingerbread with a generous stick of Gorwydd propped up against it.

GATHER COOK FEAST

Rough Apple Pie with
Walnut Raisin Caramel

SERVES 8

80g raisins
2 tablespoons Somerset Cider
    Brandy or Calvados
40g walnuts
35g butter
70g light brown sugar
a pinch of sea salt
400g of the best, most
    flavourful apples
1 tablespoon caster sugar

The pastry
200g cold unsalted butter
320g plain flour
50g caster sugar
a pinch of sea salt
1 whole egg
4–6 drops Angostura bitters
1 teaspoon cider vinegar
iced water
1 beaten egg, for glazing

The rich pastry in this recipe has a rough-and-ready, rubble-like look, the combined juices of flavourful apple and nutty caramel oozing from the cracks. I owe the talented Elsen sisters (of Four & Twenty Blackbirds fame) a credit for the idea of adding Angostura and cider vinegar to pastry: the little notes of bitterness and brightness work so well. For some tips on pastry making, see page 147.

The British Isles boasts up to two thousand apple varieties – almost all falling out of favour for commercial production. This narrowing of available varieties suits the supermarkets rather more than the cook or grower. The old varieties have magical names such as the eaters Roundway Magnum Bonum, Allington Pippin, Rosemary Russet, cookers such as Belle de Boskoop and Lord Derby, and taste wonderful.

Seek out the very best-tasting apples for this recipe – either cookers or eaters are OK. Ask for unusual varieties at your local store or farmers' market. Long live variety!

Chop the cold butter into small cubes and rub it into the flour until the mixture resembles fine breadcrumbs. Add the caster sugar and salt.

Mix the egg with the bitters and cider vinegar and blend into the pastry until the mixture forms large crumbs. Then add a tablespoon or so of iced water until the mixture starts to cling together. It's important not to overdo the water, otherwise your pastry may shrink, and given the higher proportion of butter here, plus the egg, you really won't need much water.

Combine into a large, flat bun shape, wrap in clingfilm and refrigerate for an hour or so (or overnight).

Heat the oven to 200°C/180°C fan/gas 6.

While the pastry is chilling, soak the raisins in the brandy and toast the walnuts in the oven for 8 minutes, or until golden. Rub the toasted nuts in a clean tea towel to remove as much of the bitter skin as possible, then crush them into small pieces with your hand.

Melt the butter in a non-stick pan over a medium heat, add the brown sugar and a pinch of salt and combine until the mixture bubbles away

GATHER COOK FEAST

and begins to turn a chestnut brown, looking glossy and viscous. It's important not to use too much heat here as the caramel may spoil – 1–2 minutes should do it.

Add the raisins with the brandy to the caramel mixture, together with the walnuts. Reduce the mixture for a few moments more, until slick and not too wet. Set aside until you are ready to assemble the pie.

Cover a large baking tray with baking paper.

Take the pastry from the fridge and divide into two-thirds and one-third. Roll out the larger piece on a floured surface, making a circle around 2mm thick which fits your baking tray. Place this larger circle on the paper-covered tray and brush with beaten egg to glaze.

Core, quarter and very thinly slice the apples along the length of the quarters on to the pastry base, piling the slices in the centre and leaving a gap of about 3–4cm around the edge (quick slicing of the apple avoids it browning).

Roll out the smaller piece of pastry in the same way.

Pour the caramel mixture over the top of the apple and then top with the second round of pastry. Brush the surface of the top and the exposed edges of the bottom with a little water, then bring up the edges of the bottom over the top and press down to form a seal, pleating around the circle to give a rough-hewn look.

Dust the pie lightly with a little caster sugar, slice a small hole in the top and pop into the oven for 30–35 minutes, until golden brown.

Eat the pie on its own, or with thin cream.

Spiced Orange Bitters
& Two Cocktails

MAKES 1 SMALL
BOTTLE OF BITTERS

For spiced orange bitters
1 Seville orange
250ml vodka
scant ¼ teaspoon whole cloves
scant ¼ teaspoon coriander seeds
scant ½ teaspoon black peppercorns
½ a vanilla pod, cut into several
    pieces, but left unsplit
1 green cardamom pod,
    partially cracked open
a 1cm piece of cinnamon stick
1 small blade of mace
1 roasted coffee bean

JANUARY TO FEBRUARY
FOR SEVILLE ORANGES

In the darkest part of the year the arrival of bitter, fragrant Seville oranges does much to cheer the spirit. In my home there is an obsessive desire not to miss them, which resulted in my boiling up four successive cauldrons of marmalade just when I should have been finishing this book. But Seville oranges are divine, a truly seasonal fruit, both bitter and fragrant at the same time. Put whole fruits in the freezer to extend the season. Use them instead of lemon in a salad dressing, slice them into a Negroni or a Campari and soda, grate the zest and dribble the juice over tofu or a yoghurty topping on savoury lentils.

I have always been fascinated by the botanicals used to flavour gin and vermouth. Here is a chance to play at being a master distiller by the simple addition of Seville rinds and spices to vodka. The Seville adds the bitterness more usually provided by wormwood. The suggested cocktails are strong, straight-up versions that celebrate the bitterness. Lemon Barley Mac tastes a little like lemon barley sweets and the title references Whisky Mac, the classic cocktail of whisky and ginger wine. The Sloe Winter Cup is dark, rich and fruity with spices.

Spiced Orange Bitters

MAKES 1 LARGE COCKTAIL

Heat the oven to 120°C/100°C fan/gas ½. Use a paring knife to score the rind of the orange into segments so it is easy to peel. Keep the flesh to squeeze into a salad dressing. Cut the peel into 2cm squares and spread evenly over a baking sheet. Bake in the oven for around 30 minutes, until dry but not yet brittle. Cool.

Place the dried peel in a clean jam jar along with the vodka and all the other ingredients. Seal and leave to infuse for around 3 weeks, shaking the jar from time to time.

Strain the vodka through a sieve lined with a piece of damp muslin or other fine cloth. Gather up the muslin and squeeze out the last of the vodka. Decant to a small bottle and store somewhere dark. The bitters will last for years, especially as only a teaspoon is used each time.

GATHER COOK FEAST

For lemon barley mac
50ml malt whisky
    (nothing too peaty)
25ml Cognac
12.5ml good white vermouth
12.5ml Stone's ginger wine
12.5ml gomme syrup
1 scant teaspoon spiced
    orange bitters (see opposite)
lemon zest, to garnish

Lemon Barley Mac

MAKES 1 LARGE COCKTAIL

If you can't lay your hands on gomme (also called gum) syrup, a sugar solution used for cocktails, make your own by dissolving equal volumes of sugar and water together. Cool before using. Ready-made gomme syrup will have a silkier mouth-feel, as it contains gum arabic.

Measure all the liquid ingredients into a jug filled with ice. Stir for several minutes, then strain into two small Martini glasses. Finish each glass with a small piece of lemon zest, twisted so as to spray lemon oil over the surface of the cocktail.

For sloe winter cup
50ml sloe whisky (see page 330)
25ml good bourbon
12.5ml good white vermouth
12.5ml good red vermouth
1 teaspoon spiced orange
    bitters (see opposite)
orange zest, to garnish

Sloe Winter Cup

MAKES 1 LARGE COCKTAIL

What you put into this determines the final cocktail. For an extra Christmassy feel, use Antica Formula rather than standard red vermouth.

Measure all the liquid ingredients into a jug filled with ice. Stir for several minutes, then strain into two small Martini glasses. Finish each glass with a small piece of orange zest, twisted so as to spray orange oil over the surface of the cocktail.

Sloe Whisky

MAKES AS MUCH AS YOU LIKE

sloes, stems removed and rinsed
whisky
sugar to taste

OCTOBER FOR RIPE SLOES

A subtle and lovely variation on the more usual sloe gin – you can also make sloe vodka and sloe brandy. Or try using other autumn fruit such as blackberries, haws or damsons. The method is the same in each case.

Pick plump sloes dark in colour and very slightly soft to the squeeze. Avoid green or shrivelled ones, and bushes next to busy roads or sprayed crops. It's a bit of a myth that you need to wait until the first frost – it's much more important to find perfectly ripe sloes. It's also a myth that you need to prick each sloe. Pulling out their stems breaks the skin sufficiently to release their flavour. If you prick them you risk the whisky becoming cloudy. Choose a good-quality blended whisky; there's no need for an expensive single malt.

Fill a large clean jar just over half full with sloes. Pour over whisky to almost fill the jar and add a couple of spoonfuls of sugar. If you go easy on the sugar now it's always possible to add more later if needed.

Close the jar and leave it somewhere dark for at least 3 months and preferably a year. The longer you leave the whisky on the sloes the better it will taste. The almondy flavour of the stones only comes out after time.

Strain the whisky through a sieve lined with a piece of damp muslin set over a jug. Don't squish the fruit; let it drip. Taste the whisky and stir in more sugar if needed.

Leave the whisky to settle overnight, then decant into a clean bottle, leaving the cloudy sediment behind. You can drink it straight away, but it will keep for years and improve with age.

SUPPLIERS OF UNUSUAL INGREDIENTS

Game & Mutton

— Good high street butchers (also available in
some areas via delivery service www.hubbub.co.uk)
— www.wildmeat.co.uk
— www.graigfarm.co.uk
— www.thedorsetwildboarandvenisoncompany.co.uk
— www.turnerandgeorge.co.uk
— www.blackface.co.uk
— www.heritagemeats.co.uk
— www.westcoastfoods.co.uk

Fish, Shellfish, Seafood, Samphire & Crayfish Pots

— Good high street fishmongers (also available
in some areas via delivery service www.hubbub.co.uk)
— www.thecornishfishmonger.co.uk
— www.thefishsociety.co.uk
— www.thecrayfishcompany.com

Seaweed

— Health/wholefood shops
— www.cornishseaweed.co.uk
— www.maraseaweed.com
— www.justseaweed.com

Less Common Herbs, Vegetables & Fruits
*(sorrel, chervil, wild garlic, spring/summer greens,
mini cucumbers, radicchio, wet garlic, horseradish, quince)*

— Good high street greengrocers (also available
in some areas via delivery service www.hubbub.co.uk)
— www.riverford.co.uk
— www.finefoodspecialist.co.uk
— Garden centres

Edible Flowers

— www.maddocksfarmorganics.co.uk
— www.herbsunlimited.co.uk
— www.greensofdevon.com
— Garden centres

Dried Peas & Beans
(Carlin peas, runner beans, red haricot beans)

— Health/wholefood shops
— www.hodmedods.co.uk
— www.souschef.co.uk

Flours & Baking Ingredients
(bread flours, pasta flour, chestnut flour, barley flour, malt extract, sourdough starter)

— Health/wholefood shops
— www.shipton-mill.com
— www.bakerybits.co.uk
— www.dovesfarm.co.uk
— www.hobbshousebakery.co.uk
— www/souschef.co.uk
— And see the list of British flour mills here:
  www.sourdough.co.uk/british-artisan-flour-mills-by-region/

Charcuterie
(smoked pancetta, morcilla, cooking chorizo, smoked pork/ham ribs, British charcuterie)

— Good high street butchers and delis (also available in some areas via delivery service www.hubbub.co.uk)
— www.trealyfarm.com
— www.cannonandcannon.com
— www.dorsetcharcuterie.co.uk
— www.westcoastfoods.co.uk
— www.brindisa.com
— www.purespain.co.uk
— www.thetapaslunchcompany.co.uk

Curing, Smoking &
Sausage-making Supplies

(wood dusts, hog casings, etc.)

— www.weschenfelder.co.uk
— www.hotsmoked.co.uk
— www.homecuring.co.uk
— www.sausagemaking.org
— www.lakeland.co.uk
— www.souschef.co.uk

Unusual Spices, Condiments
& Other Ingredients

(black cardamom, fenugreek, violet olives, preserved lemons, Shaoxing wine, coarse polenta, etc.)

— Good high street delis (also available in some
  areas via delivery service www.hubbub.co.uk)
— www.souschef.co.uk
— www.ottolenghi.co.uk
— www.spicesofindia.co.uk

FURTHER READING & LEARNING

Foraging

Marjorie Blamey & Christopher Grey-Wilson, *Wild Flowers of Britain and Northern Europe*, Cassell, 1974

Alys Fowler, *The Thrifty Forager: living off your local landscape*, Kyle Books, 2015

Patience Gray, *Honey from a Weed: fasting and feasting in Tuscany, Catalonia, the Cyclades and Apulia*, Prospect Books, 1986

* Fiona Houston and Xa Milne, *Seaweed and Eat It: a family foraging and cooking adventure*, Virgin Books, 2008

* Miles Irving, *The Forager Handbook: a guide to the edible plants of Britain*, Ebury Press, 2009

Richard Mabey, *Food for Free: a guide to the edible wild plants of Britain*, HarperCollins, 1972

Roger Phillips, *Mushrooms & Other Funghi of Great Britain and Europe*, Pan, 1981

* Roger Phillips, *Wild Food: a complete guide for foragers*, Orbis, 2014

Vivien Weise, *Cooking Weeds: a vegetarian cookery book*, Prospect Books, 2009

John Wright, *Hedgerow: River Cottage Handbook No. 7*, River Cottage, 2014

More Information & Courses on Foraging

Around Britain – www.foragingcourses.com

Miles Irving – www.forager.org.uk

John Wright – www.wild-food.net

Preservation, Fermentation & Curing

* Pam Corbin, *Preserves: River Cottage Handbook No. 2*, River Cottage, 2008

Diana Henry, *Salt Sugar Smoke: how to preserve fruit, vegetables, meat and fish*, Mitchell Beazley, 2012

* Sandor Katz, *Wild Fermentation: the flavour, nutrition and craft of live culture foods*, Chelsea Green, 2003, www.wildfermentation.com

* Marguerite Patten, *Jams, Preserves and Chutneys*, National Trust, 1995

The gardeners and farmers of Centre Terre Vivante, *Preserving Food without Freezing or Canning*, Chelsea Green, 1999

More Information & Courses on Preservation, Fermentation & Curing

Anna Colquhoun – www.culinaryanthropologist.org
Tiffany Jesse – www.themirabelletree.com

Breadmaking

Richard Bertinet, *Crust: from sourdough, spelt and rye bread*, Kyle Cathie, 2012
* Richard Bertinet, *Dough: simple contemporary bread*, Kyle Cathie, 2008
Justin Gellatly, *Bread, Cake, Doughnut, Pudding*, Fig Tree, 2014
Jeffrey Hamelman, *Bread: a baker's book of techniques and recipes*, John Wiley & Sons, 2004
Dan Lepard, *The Handmade Loaf: contemporary recipes for the home baker*, Octopus, 2004
* Chad Robertson, *Tartine Bread*, Chronicle Books, 2010
Daniel Stevens, *Bread: River Cottage Handbook No. 3*, River Cottage, 2009
Andrew Whitley, *Bread Matters*, Fourth Estate, 2006

More Information & Courses on Breadmaking

Richard Bertinet – www.thebertinetkitchen.com
Vanessa Kimbell – www.sourdough.co.uk
Andrew Whitley – www.breadmatters.com

More About Sustainable Fish & Fishing

Good Fish Guide – www.goodfishguide.org
Greenpeace – www.greenpeace.org.uk/oceans/what-you-can-do/better-buys-what-fish-can-I-eat
Marine Conservation Society – www.mcsuk.org
Oceana – www.oceana.org
Sustainable Seafood Coalition – www.sustainableseafoodcoalition.org

General Reading

Alexandra Harris, *Weatherland: writers and artists under English skies*, Thames & Hudson, 2015

Professor Dan Jurafsky, *The Language of Food: a linguist reads the menu*, W. W. Norton, 2014

Harold McGee, *On Food and Cooking: the science and lore of the kitchen*, Scribner, 1984

George Monbiot, *Feral: searching for enchantment on the frontiers of re-wilding*, Penguin, 2013

Michael Pollan, *Cooked: a natural history of transformation*, Allen Lane, 2013

Colin Spencer, *From Microliths to Microwaves: the evolution of British agriculture, food and cooking*, Grub Street, 2011

Maguelonne Toussaint-Samat, *History of Food*, Wiley Blackwell, 1992

* Especially recommended

BIOGRAPHIES

Jessica Seaton studied Ancient History & Archaeology at Birmingham University, before starting her own knitwear business with her husband, Jamie. But she is better known as one of the two founders of TOAST, a leading British fashion and lifestyle brand.

As an enthusiastic cook she enjoys creating new meals for family and friends. She divides her time between working in London and her home in West Wales, where she has a thriving kitchen garden and often walks the hills looking for foraged produce.

She uses her blog and Instagram to photograph and write about landscape, food and a sense of place.

Anna Colquhoun is a food anthropologist, consultant, writer and cooking teacher who has travelled widely through Europe, the Middle East and West Africa understanding local cuisines. Anna trained as a chef in San Francisco and at Alice Waters's legendary restaurant Chez Panisse.

She is the author of *Eat Slow Britain* and a consultant on BBC Radio 4's *The Kitchen Cabinet*. In her spare time she is renovating a beautiful stone farmhouse in Croatia.

INDEX

ACKNOWLEDGEMENTS

Although years in the making, the heaviest work on this book fell during a period of intense activity in my day job, when each week brought new challenges and every weekend was devoted to recipe testing. Realizing I was the main cook, my husband, Jamie, graciously stepped aside to allow me to undertake this project on my own (the first time in our working life where we have worked separately). Without his support I may never have had the courage to do this. During this time, he was forced to put up with a largely absent wife and patiently withstood any fallout that came his way. My boundless love and thanks to you, Jamie.

To my children, Rachel and Nick, thank you for your unquestioning support, recipe testing, and for your sage advice. You are both tremendous and I love you deeply. Thank you also, Nicko, for your beautiful landscape pictures. I loved working with you on those. Thanks also to Nat for many perfectly made Negronis when I most needed them, and to the beautiful Athelstan, the light of all our lives.

To Anna Colquhoun, thank you for your help in this whole project, for answering queries while juggling building works and for your spirit – you know you are good.

To my friends and family, who ate the food, put up with mistakes, mopped me up when the going got tough and said the nicest things – William and Lynne Wilkins, Sian and Bruce Collins, Liz and Boyd Webb, Jo and Orlando Gough and my lovely sister Kate. Also thanks to Simon, Maryann and Joel Wright, Richard and Matt (thanks for the preserved lemons and sauerkraut chat, Matt) and everyone at Wright's who fed me and poured me delicious natural wines when I couldn't cook any more.

Very special thanks are due to Orlando Gough, whose faith in me as a cook led him to dedicate his own recipe book to me – perhaps the moment when I had the first sideways glimmer of confidence in my abilities – and who generously offered testing and overall advice on the book as a whole. You are a true friend and fellow food-lover.

Thanks are also due to Neil Williams, the nicest man in the world, who gave me the time to devote to this project.

I couldn't have done this at all if it were not for the faith shown in me by Lizzy Kremer, my agent. You are a very special person – thank you. Thanks too to the whole team at David Higham, and especially Harriet, whose tolerance of my forgetfulness is, it seems, limitless.

It has been a pleasure to get to know the team at Fig Tree, especially Juliet Annan, whose company I really value, whose advice and knowledge of publishing command deep respect and whom I would like to call my friend. Thank you for your support of this project, I have loved working with you. Thanks also to Anna Steadman and Annie Lee – professional and lovely, both.

The whole process of photographing the food was an especial joy for me, so similar and yet so different to the shoots I do for TOAST. It has been a privilege to work with the whole team. Sophie Missing, who is the most unflappable cook I know, Juliet for her stalwart washing up and foraging skills and, most of all, Jonathan Lovekin for his calm and amazing photography. Thank you all.

To Akiko Hirai and to Ana at Kana who generously sent in plates and bowls for the shoot, your work is awesome and you have beautiful hearts, thank you.

To Charlotte Heal who designed the finished book, your design makes the world a better place. Thank you.

So many people have been generous with information and their time: the team at Natoora and the Fish Society; my local butchers Dewi Roberts and Julian Cooper; Towy Fishmonger; my friend and mushroom forager Phil Roberts (who answered the call for a basket of sloes and wild mushrooms); my neighbour Jim who brings the muck to nourish the veggies; Ben and Mike who hoe and plant; Hils who arranges all homely matters; and finally Hilary and Hugh Jones who filled my freezer with their delicious Berkshire pork one weekend. You are unsung heroes and part of making this book what it is. Thank you all.

Last, but not least, thank you to all those who buy this book, follow me on Instagram or read my blog posts. You all support me and I appreciate it deeply.